PRAISE FOR PROSPERITY NOW!

"*Prosperity Now!* will have you thinking in new, life-changing, life-affirming ways that will help you get out of your own way so prosperity can make its way through to you. Thank you, John Frederick, for this game-changer!"

— Tyler R. Tichelaar, PhD and award-winning author of *Narrow Lives* and *The Best Place* (Marquette, MI)

"With humor and grounded spirituality, John Frederick encourages us to follow Thoreau's advice and go confidently in the direction of our dreams. His book is rich in personal stories as well as practical exercises for setting intentions for a more abundant life—intentions the body can believe and that may engage the support of greater powers. John's willingness to share the thrills and spills of his own life odyssey—climbing up from the pit of despair and homeless addiction to a dream life in Paris as *flâneur*, musician, writer, and motivational speaker—lends authenticity to this contemporary version of *Think and Grow Rich*."

— Robert Moss, bestselling author of *Conscious Dreaming, The Secret History of Dreaming,* and *Dreaming the Soul Back Home* (New York)

"The *Prosperity Now!* sessions have been a mind and heart opening experience. They have opened my vision of what abundance truly is and what living a successful life means to me personally. I took the course twice and got different information each time. This step-by-step approach is very well put together: clearly and progressively. John's life experiences illustrate every point in a real and lively manner. I highly recommend the book or the coaching sessions. They have changed my life."

— Maylin Pultar, international singer-songwriter, world music performer (Paris, France)

"In *Prosperity Now!* John provides wonderful and accessible, real-world examples of how the universal laws work, along with ways we can utilize those laws to create our best and fullest lives. This book is a necessary tool for everyone."

— Jennifer Selkirk, special education teacher and *Prosperity Now!* student (Albany, NY)

"*Prosperity Now!* by Rev John Frederick is destined to become a prosperity classic. The book is a masterful blending of Twelve Step work, *A Course in Miracles*, New Thought, Taoism, and more. John's accounts of his personal experiences along the journey to a prosperous life, along with stories and comments from others, keeps the book engaging from beginning to end. *Prosperity Now!* is a great resource for those seeking to create a more prosperous and fulfilling life, as well as those of us looking for some inspiration and tools for stepping up our prosperity."

— Rev. Jim & Rev. Kay Fuller (Charlotte, NC)

"Over the years, I have watched John Frederick from a distance as he manifested his dreams in ways that appeared to be miraculous. Having read *Prosperity Now!*, I now believe the "miracles" are a result of several actions: surrendering unhelpful thoughts and beliefs, "seeing things right" not "setting them right," and a readiness to accept that the wisdom and beneficence of the universe is within one's self. His methodic, step-by-Twelve-Step principle approach using real life success stories is an effective tool for readers who desire to manifest their dreams."

— Dottie Frament, OTR, BCST, LMT,
and *Prosperity Now!* student (Albany, NY)

"*Prosperity Now!* has been a life-changing blessing. I realized for years that the Robin deep down inside was desperate for change, but also I knew a change was not going to happen. I was endlessly going in circles. *Prosperity Now!* appeared in a random moment of clarity while my father was visiting from Paris for Christmas! I admired his serenity, and I desperately wished I had my life as together as he did. In that moment, I decided I was ready to finally listen to my inner wisdom: *Now is your moment, Robin!* I recently finished the course. I am going through new awakenings, and inside, I know the transformation is happening. I feel myself awakening and my mind opening up to thoughts, beliefs, and emotions I would have either dismissed before or I was to blind to appreciate. The process is a new, amazing part of my life, and being able to be a part of such a wonderful experience with my father as my mentor is something I cannot even put into words!"

— Robin DeFilipo, teacher
and *Prosperity Now!* student (Long Island, NY)

"John Frederick has masterfully designed a book that aligns your heart and soul into manifesting a life of prosperity, abundance, and fulfillment. *Prosperity Now! A 12-Week Journey to the Life of Your Dreams* takes you on an amazing weekly journey through the use of personal stories, his own and those of others, spiritual teachings, and the principles of prosperity. I really loved the opportunity to use it for self-reflection. If you want to change your life and your attitude, this is the book for you!"
— Diane Albano, Ed.D, life coach, speaker, author of *The Art of Being Nice*, and *Prosperity Now!* student (Albany, NY)

"John Frederick's *"Prosperity Now!"* is a transformational twelve-week journey you will take to tune into your prosperous mind. It's insightful, profound, and life-changing. I have had many aha moments throughout the course, a lot of confirmations, and wonderful insights. I am very thankful and blessed to have taken part in this wonderful journey. I would recommend it to anyone who wishes to change their life for the better and start living in abundance."
— Maja Savić, holistic coach & healer, jazz vocalist, voice coach, meditation teacher, founder of QInspired Life, and *Prosperity Now!* student (Paris, France)

"My dear, good brother John introduced me to his course with its warm and loving spiritual insights on how the universe is filled with abundance! *Prosperity Now!* is for me a way to redirect my thoughts and mind, and tune into the abundance of the universe. John has mastered this in a very spiritual and loving way that builds foundations of peace within, and that is rooted deeply in the soul of gratitude. My life is filled with happiness and abundance."
— Ladell McLin, international blues musician, singer-songwriter, music producer, and *Prosperity Now!* student (Paris, France)

"*Prosperity Now!* contains valuable keys that create a consciousness of prosperity, which leads to the experience of a most rewarding life. John Frederick beautifully blends wisdom from his own lived experience and from the great teachers of our time to create a common sense approach that helps transform a mentality of lack to a mentality of sufficiency and prosperity."
— Sam House, MCC, CPCC (Delmar, NY)

"*Prosperity Now*'s twelve-week program will help many people for years to come. The use of the Twelve Steps as a framework is powerful and effective. For people unfamiliar with the Twelve Step spiritual program, this is a good introduction. John's personal testimony gives the course strength and authenticity. In the book, I especially enjoyed John's travels to Paris, the Waldorf Salad story, and the NYC Thanksgiving Parade story. As a teacher of Interfaith students at a seminary, I found the use of Interfaith quotes and affirmations most beneficial."
— Rev. Dr. Kathleen T. Regan, Dean, All Faiths Seminary International (New York, NY)

"*Prosperity Now!* is a wonderful book to help guide you to live a more abundant, joyous, and prosperous life. John has followed his dreams and his heart, and is now living in Paris. Perhaps your dreams will lead you there too! I highly recommend that you pick up this book!"
— Zara Durrani, TV host, producer, Parisian & world traveler (Vancouver, Canada)

"*Prosperity Now* is a gem for all who seek to live their everyday lives from a place of life-affirming prosperity consciousness. John Frederick's personal life experiences and profound healing path are perhaps the most compelling testimony about the power and integrity of this book's prosperity principles. John's weave of great teachings with practical every day application has been life-changing. Thank you, John!"
— Heather Diddel, Attorney and *Prosperity Now!* student

PROSPERITY NOW!

A 12-WEEK JOURNEY TO THE LIFE OF YOUR DREAMS

John A. Frederick

PROSPERITY NOW!
A 12-WEEK JOURNEY TO THE LIFE OF YOUR DREAMS

Second Edition - Copyright © 2021 by John Frederick. All rights reserved.

Published by: John A. Frederick

All Rights Reserved. No part of this book may be used or reproduced in any manner whatsoever without the expressed written permission of the author except for brief quotations in reviews or scholarly articles.

Prosperity Now© is also a copyrighted term and cannot be used without written permission of the author.

Address all inquiries to:

John A. Frederick

911 Central Avenue, Box 205

Albany, NY 12206

prosperitynowlifeofdreams@yahoo.com

www.prosperitynowlifeofdreams.com

ISBN: 978-1-7351158-2-5

Library of Congress Control Number: 2020909655

Editors: Tyler Tichelaar and Larry Alexander, Superior Book Productions

Cover Design and Interior Book Layout: Larry Alexander, Superior Book Productions

Author Photo Credit: John A. Frederick

Every attempt has been made to properly source all quotes.

Printed in the United States of America

To my daughters, Nicole and Robin,
and to my granddaughter, Nevaeh Nicole.

May these spiritual principles enlighten your way,
lighten your path, and help you make your light shine even brighter.

Acknowledgments

With deepest gratitude to:

My original *Prosperity Now!* course students: Robin DeFilipo, Mark Johnson, Ladell McLin, Vanessa Paris, Maylin Pultar, and Maja Savic.

My original *Prosperity Now!* group at Unity Church in Albany, and to Unity Church in Albany, where I first encountered metaphysical spiritual principles and where I was able to work on this manuscript.

Dr. Diane Albano, Rev. Jim Fuller, Rev. Crystal Muldrow, Donna Reed, and Rev. Arthur Wells for editing, encouraging, and teaching prosperity principles to me.

My fellow classmates at All-Faiths Seminary International, Rev. Kay Fuller, Rev. Roger Mock, and Rev. Barbara Sinacore, as well as our teachers and mentors, Rev. Jon Mundy and Rev. Dr. Kathleen Regan.

The other members of my "Spiritual Board of Directors," Gregory Anderson, Sylvia Conant, Keri Chryst, Tony DelPozzo, Dot Dugan, Jim E., Paul G., Robert Moss, and Lynn Stone.

My editors, Tyler Tichelaar and Larry Alexander at Superior Book Productions.

Rob Brezsny for introducing me to the term, "Pronoia" and permission to use his quote.

Karen Drucker for permission to reproduce her lyrics to "I Am So Blessed."

Rhonda Findling for permission to use her quote from The Daily Om.

Robert Moss for permission to use the excerpt from his essay on his book, "The Three Only Things."

Mark Shepard for permission to use his question from his talk, "Why does this work out better than I can possibly imagine?"

Unity Unity®, publisher of Daily Word®, for permission to reprint the poem "Child of Light" by Martha Smock.

Andrews McMeer Syndication for permission to reprint the Calvin and Hobbes cartoon.

Alcoholics Anonymous Worldwide for permission to reprint the Twelve Steps of Alcoholics Anonymous. The Twelve Steps of Alcoholics Anonymous are reprinted and adapted with permission of Alcoholics Anonymous World Services, Inc. ("A. A. W. S.") Permission to adapt the Twelve Steps does not mean that A. A. W. S. has reviewed or approved the contents of this publication, or that A. A. W. S. necessarily agrees with the views expressed herein. A. A. is a program of recovery from alcoholism only—use of the Twelve Steps in connection with programs and activities which are patterned after A. A., but which address other problems, or in any other non-A. A. context, does not imply otherwise.

Excerpts From A Course In Miracles ((Original Edition)) Helen Schucman, Anonymous & William Thetford.

A Course in Miracles is a public domain document, and the reader is free to read, enjoy, and share all or any part of it without the permission of any person.

To hear Karen Drucker's song, "I Am So Blessed" which accompanies each week's tithing, go to https://youtu.be/2SHaEjFtP2g

Contents

Preface i
Week 1: Surrender to Win 1
Week 2: Change Your Thinking to Change Your Life 21
Week 3: Happy, Joyous, and Free! 37
Week 4: Stepping Out of Your Comfort Zone 53
Week 5: Begin It Now (and Don't Ask How) 69
Week 6: The Power of Gratitude and Prayer 87
Week 7: Imagination: Putting Wings on Your Dreams 103
Week 8: Imagination, Intuition, and "Creative Waiting" 119
Week 9: Defenselessness Is Safety 139
Week 10: Beyond the Limits of Your Sight 157
Week 11: Goals, Shamans, and the Mind of the Heart 175
Week 12: Your Spiritual Awakening 193
Appendix 213
About the Author 215
Book John to Speak at Your Next Event 217

Preface

LIKE ALL DIVINELY inspired ideas, Prosperity Now! started as a small seed, barely discernible amid all the noise of the world. A similar process occurred when I found myself leading tour groups to my spiritual home, Paris, France, when I had no plans to do so.

My good friend, Lois Crommelin, was talking to me about my most recent trip and she said, *"Oh I would love to go to Paris!"*

I said, *"Well.... Go!"*

She said, *"I could never go to Paris."*

I said, *"Why not?"*

She said, *"I wouldn't know how. I wouldn't know what to do when I got there."*

I said (kiddingly), *"Well, if you want to pay my way, I'll take you and show you around."*

And she said, *"Maybe we could get a group together."*

The next thing I knew, I had fliers printed, had priced out airfare and hotels, had priced in a little more to pay for my trip and—*Voila!*—Lois and another dozen people signed up and paid me to take them to Paris. Then (gulp!), I had to take them there and see that they had a good time!

That same process happened with this course, one I had no intention of creating, much less publishing as a book.

A new Parisian friend was telling me about her precarious living and financial situation. I told her of my experiences healing my own past, my financial traumas, and other dysfunctional beliefs, using spiritual principles. With them, I have had a miraculous journey from poverty and fear into prosperity and abundance. I said I would guide her if she was willing.

She was, so I started writing Week 1. To stay ahead, I immediately started Week 2. And so on.... Now, after working with some two dozen students, the result is (gulp!) this book/course.

In 2018, I moved to Paris to live out the third half of my life in early retirement. My life today is the result of working prosperity principles for twenty-five years. But it wasn't always so. Between age thirty and thirty-seven, my life tumbled completely out of control. I was homeless twice; I had had cars repossessed. I was asked to leave jobs and was virtually unemployable. I was in ill health with a very bad back and teeth falling out. I had undiagnosed HIV and was on the verge of full-blown AIDS. I had no money, few friends, no direction, and no clue.... Life did not work for me, and it was everyone's and everything's fault—but my own.

When I hit bottom, I was spiritually, financially, physically, mentally, emotionally, and psychically bankrupt. In despair, I turned to twelve-step recovery, and from that decision, a whole new world opened for me—not immediately, of course, but over time. I found people and places that were teaching and living lives according to spiritual laws that worked!

In a little more than twenty years, I went from being a twice homeless drunk/drug-addict to being a gainfully employed legislative Chief of Staff in the New York State Assembly. I was clean and sober. I owned my own home (eventually two). I was now healing—and thriving—through life's ups and downs, including a 1996 HIV diagnosis and a 2016 cancer diagnosis, a marriage and a divorce.

I credit the Innate Wisdom of the Universe, which resides in me (and in each and every one of us), for guiding me (sometimes not so gently) toward my Highest Good. I began to experience what Henry David Thoreau spoke about in his book *Walden*:

> I learned this, at least, by my experiment: that if one advances confidently in the direction of his dreams, and endeavors to live the life which he has imagined, he will meet with a success unexpected in common hours. *He will put some things behind, will pass an invisible boundary; new, universal, and more liberal*

laws will begin to establish themselves around and within him; or the old laws be expanded, and interpreted in his favor in a more liberal sense, and he will live with the license of a higher order of beings. In proportion as he simplifies his life, the laws of the universe will appear less complex, and solitude will not be solitude, nor poverty poverty, nor weakness weakness. If you have built castles in the air, your work need not be lost; that is where they should be. Now put the foundations under them.

One important pillar that buttresses and makes my new life possible—and which is the foundation of Prosperity Now!—is tithing. This, above all, is a tithe-based program. You could learn and practice all the spiritual principles in the course and you would gain some wisdom and understanding, up to a point. But the action of tithing fundamentally changes your consciousness—moving it away from thoughts of fear and lack to abundance and sufficiency.

Tithing (fully explained in Week 1) is without a doubt the greatest vehicle I know of. It will break up old fear-based thinking, replacing it *in real-time* with joyous feelings of abundance and *"the peace that passes all understanding."* The sincere and consistent tither will come to see that they are fully supported by the Universe and have nothing to fear.

The course was originally designed to be done with a teacher or guide, or in a larger church group. That is still the best way to approach it. The energy of "two or more" working together to uplift their consciousness from lack and fear to abundance and faith is unequaled. A healing energy resonates and expands whenever like-minded people gather to love and support each other.

However, the book can also be used for self-study. The mindful student will want to first discern where their tithes should go. The general rule is to the places, institutions, and people who are feeding you spiritually. Where do you get your spiritual nourishment? That is where you should direct your tithing.

To make your commitment to the course, your tithing, and the promise of your own greater happiness official, I have inserted a contract for you to make with yourself and God on the next page.

I know, without a doubt, that anyone can live the life of their dreams. No dream is unworthy or too big. If you can believe it, you can achieve it. I hope to meet some of you and hear your stories of how you dreamed bigger dreams and worked with spiritual laws to make them come true.

We are so Blessed! Thank you, God!

John A. Frederick
Paris, France

PROSPERITY NOW!

My Contract with My Self and with God

*I came that they may have life,
and that they may have it abundantly.*
— *John 10:10*

I, _____, am committed to changing my life and to opening my consciousness to the Infinite Abundance of the Universe, which is mine to enjoy.

To achieve the results I desire, I hereby commit to:

- Complete the twelve-week sessions
- Doing the **Prosperity Now!** work, readings, and homework
- Tithing to the place where I receive spiritual nourishment. For the next twelve weeks of **Prosperity Now!**, I commit to tithing ten percent (10%) of whatever income flows to me—from all sources—while I am in the course.

I understand that my willingness to open my mind to the Greater Good available to us all is key to growing an awakened and vibrant Prosperity Consciousness.

I understand that as I change my inner thoughts, beliefs, and ideas about what is true, my outer world will adjust and expand to fill my new and expanded consciousness.

I also understand that all tithes of my income to the **Prosperity Now!** course will be tracked, and if, after the completion of all twelve weeks of the course, I am not fully satisfied with my results, my tithes will be cheerfully refunded.

Signed _____ Date_____

Prosperity Now! Facilitator _____
(If being done in a church program or with another group)

Week 1

Surrender to Win

We are sure God wants us to be happy, joyous and free.
— Alcoholics Anonymous
(hereafter referred to as *The Big Book*)

*I came that they may have life,
and that they may have it abundantly.*
— John 10:10

PROSPERITY NOW! is not a way to magically manifest money. *Prosperity Now!* is much more and much deeper. Call it a "perfectly planned path for prosperity." Prosperity means many good things, which all together add up to a full life.

It is your time to prosper! That time is now! If it was not your time, you wouldn't be here. Something pulled you, called you, and you listened.

Why *Prosperity Now!* with an exclamation point? Because we are going to learn to see that our good is here, now. Now! Not in some misty past or in some distant future. The only time is now. Past and future live outside of present reality and exist (if at all) only in our minds.

A woman at my church once prayed with me about a dilemma I was facing, and she kept saying it was resolved, now. She kept seeing and saying that the prayer was answered, now. And she really shouted out the "now."

The point is you can only change now. That is your place of power....

This course is all about retraining our perceptions so we see reality in spirit and in truth. A big part of that shift is "to put our head where our feet are," and live in the present, seeing past appearances. Seeing everything around us as if our good has already arrived!

Learning how to listen to our intuition is another big part of this course. It is the guide that will never fail you. So is taking action. Nothing will really change until new action is taken. You cannot learn to swim by reading about swimming. You must get in the water and take your feet off the bottom of the pool if you want to learn to swim in prosperity.

So, let's first honor your process that brought you here. Maybe it seemed random. Maybe it was out of a crisis or desperation. Maybe it was out of curiosity. Maybe it was from a deep longing for something better than what you have been experiencing up until now.

Whatever it was, honor yourself and congratulate yourself for courage, for willingness, and for a sense of adventure—an inner adventure. A large part of what we will be doing is looking inward, seeing and examining our thinking, our current life, our present situation.

One truth we will continue to reinforce throughout the course is that our outer circumstances are just a reflection of our inner state of being. You may not believe that right now, but we will go deeper into that concept through this course.

What Is Prosperity?

Often, people automatically think "money" or "wealth" when they think about prosperity and abundance. Finances are a part of prosperity—and we will do much work in the realm of money (which is, like all things, really a spiritual energy). We work with money because the world attaches so much baggage, fear, and importance to money.

But true prosperity involves so much more than money. A sole focus on finances will cheat you out of a full life and all the good the Universe has in store for you, and that you deserve.

The thesaurus' synonyms for "prosperity" are "flourishing, successful, affluent, thriving, wellness, expansion, luxury, opulence, plenty, health, fortune, wholeness, etc."

Through the spiritual tool of tithing, we use money, but it is merely our vehicle to rocket us into a higher plane—of peace, serenity, ease, joy, happiness, usefulness to others, and most of all, a deeper spiritual life.

To achieve greater monetary wealth without an increase in spiritual gifts—like love, compassion, generosity, forgiveness, patience, serenity, or other "fruits of the Spirit"—is, at best, a hollow victory. At worst, it can be a curse. Anyone who watches the news regularly can tell you about seemingly wealthy people who are very unhappy, and who end up destroying their lives.

True prosperity encompasses a wealth (pun intended) of things that make our time on this planet joyous and complete. Some of the things you will want to include in your prosperity are:

- ☐ A functional, loving family
- ☐ An abundance of good friends
- ☐ Joyous employment or other productive activities
- ☐ Good physical, mental, and emotional health
- ☐ A spirit of generosity
- ☐ Peace of mind (serenity)
- ☐ Healthy, healing laughter
- ☐ Helping to create a better world
- ☐ An abundance of love from Source—and from the many channels of supply

Add your ideas of what a prosperous, abundant, full life looks like:

_____
_____
_____
_____
_____
_____

Surrender

The first thing we must do on our journey is—Surrender. That's right. Put your hands up and say, *"I give up!"*

"I surrender" is freeing. It is liberating and necessary when starting a journey on a new path to break free of our old thinking.

Face it; the old path was a dead end, or you would still enjoy being on it. It would still work. And if it used to work, it stopped working.

A new journey requires a giving up of the old ways...of thinking.

We surrender to the fact that the way we have been living and what we have been *experiencing* has been (at best) less than ideal. At some level, we want freedom and joy, but instead, we have lack and limitation. As we will see, our life is a direct result of our thinking.

Lack and limitation *without* points directly to thoughts (deep, often unconscious thoughts) of lack and limitation *within*.

Step 1— We admitted we were powerless over our old consciousness of lack and limitation—that our lives had become unmanageable.

The first step on our journey is, of course, Step 1. It says we know we are powerless.

Over twelve weeks, we will take advantage of one of the greatest gifts ever to be given to humankind, the twelve-step recovery program. This program started with alcoholics in the 1930s in the United States, and it has spread all over the world, expanding to encompass all types of addictions and dysfunctional ways of thinking and behaving.

If you are not familiar with the steps of recovery, know that they have helped millions to live better lives—freer, richer, saner, more productive, and amazing lives. "Extraordinary ordinary" lives as they say.

The twelve steps will work for you, too, if you follow the path laid down by countless others ahead of you and do a few simple things.

Simple, but not easy.

In twelve-step recovery, we learn we can't solve a problem unless we first admit there is a problem, and we surrender—not fight. The reality of our current situation, and more importantly, our current way of thinking, is what we surrender to. We are powerless to change it all by ourselves.

Only when we are *aware* of the problem and *accept* that we have a problem can we then begin to take action!

Surrender begins when we notice our life is not what we want, not what we had hoped. However, rather than try to rearrange people, places, and things outside of us, we begin to pay attention to our thinking and our feelings—to our inner landscape.

We begin to notice our thoughts and start to question them. We ask:

- Why do I believe that?
- Where did I get that belief from?
- How do I know that's true?
- That used to work, but it hasn't for a long time. Why do I still say/think/do that?

Taking the first step means surrendering to the fact that maybe—just maybe—our old thoughts need to be examined carefully and maybe—just maybe—they need to be thrown out altogether...or at the very least, they need an upgrade.

The rest of the program will help us to notice, question, and modify—or jettison—our old thoughts and to train our minds to replace them with higher level thinking.

Appearances Are Deceiving

A higher order of thinking starts by questioning our responses or reactions to an event and moving our thoughts to a higher plane.

> *"Do not judge according to appearances
> but use right judgment."*
> — John 7:24

Surrendering what we think about an event shifts our mind away from how things *seem* to look (appearances) toward the way they *really* are in spiritual reality.

A modern way to state this concept is: *Looks can be deceiving.*

We see or experience something and right away our mind fills in the blanks. It super-imposes old experiences over the present moment because the experiences seem similar. We react rather than pause. We react from a place of fear.

When we surrender to our old habitual ways, we can think, listen, and then act from a place of power.

We think we see what we see and hear what we hear. But we superimpose our own "spin" on people, places, and events.

The Truth Is: We see things not as *they* are, but *as we are*. Therefore, appearances are deceiving. Throughout our course, we will come back to this idea and learn how to see things rightly. To "judge with right judgment."

Set It Right or See It Right?

A good way to remind ourselves of this shift is to apply this truth in any difficult situation: "Our job is not to set things right, but to *see* things right."

We want to feel safe. For the ego, that often means controlling people, places, and things. Our natural inclination is to get a person, place, or thing to "behave." If we can rearrange things to our liking, then all will be well, we think.

But when the *Titanic* is going down, rearranging the deck chairs is futile. No amount of willpower, grit, and determination will halt the slide. Like grasping water, all will slip through our fingers. Then what?

As we look at what brought us to *Prosperity Now!*—wanting a better life; wanting to walk a spiritual path—many of us see we didn't even consider changing until something dramatic or even tragic happened. Something arose, jarring us out of our complacency and onto another path.

We may have had a sudden, serious realignment of our whole world, an experience many call a...

Crash and Burn

Alistair Hardy, a marine biologist who wrote The Spiritual Nature of Man and who founded the Religious Experience Research Center, studied thousands of people who had mystical experiences, shifts in consciousness, and/or deepening faith and beliefs. He found that over 80 percent of them came to their awakening via a "crash and burn" experience: a major or a series of major life catastrophe(s).

Their life strategies failed them. Their most cherished beliefs were proven to be hollow. Their reliance on a spouse, business, their bodies, or society let them down hard.

When life (which is consciousness) leads us down dead-end paths, when our plans don't pan out, when a marriage fails, when illness comes, when a job becomes a trap, when we hit a crisis—we are given a great gift in the midst of tragedy or calamity or when we are stuck in the doldrums of life....

We have an opportunity to throw away the old to make room for the new!

That is surrender. Put down your rusty, tired armor; let down your defenses. Join the winning side. Often, only a Gift of Desperation (G.O.D.) will motivate us to make radical changes and accept new ideas.

Before we hit the wall, we may believe our thinking is okay, even great. We may not recognize how miserable we really are. We may be satisfied with crumbs, thinking we're getting cake.

We hit bottom, and we admit that maybe, just maybe, we are part of the problem. Our decisions based on our thinking got us to where we are right now. At least in part.

And we are ready for change! So, we surrender. We admit that our thinking causes our circumstances.

What is needed then is action. We need to learn practical ways that train our mind to turn away from old, limiting thoughts and toward a higher level of thinking, which we can, in fact, learn, practice, and develop.

As I said, we often come to surrender through crisis. A twelve-step sponsor of mine, Jim E., once told me, "Just when I thought my life was falling apart, that was when it was really all coming together."

You see, the appearance that everything is going to hell is scary... and sad. The marriage is over; the job is over; the health crisis seems insurmountable; the kids are in trouble; the dog died; the house is in foreclosure, etc., etc.

That's only appearance!

Turning away from what meets the eye and looking at life with an inward, spiritual eye, we will see a bigger picture. A truer picture.

Like Kris Kristofferson wrote, and Janis Joplin sang, *Freedom is having nothing left to lose.* Ain't that the truth? Seeing things correctly means freedom from troubles, fears, and worries.

When all seems lost, we can choose to sink into despair and depression. Or we can look past appearances with new eyes. We will find that we are free, unencumbered. The world and our lives are a clean slate on which to write.

Bill Watterson's comic strip, *Calvin and Hobbes*, ended on New Year's Eve, 1995. Its ending was timed to align with the day when we pause, take stock, reflect backward, and look forward. The last strip profoundly illustrates the power of endings—which are always beginnings....[1]

It is a magical world when we stop seeing things the old way and look through fresh, spiritual eyes that see things not as they appear to be, but as they really are!

Affirmations

One of the most powerful ways to change our thinking from lack and limitation to prosperity consciousness is by using positive affirmations, affirmative expressions of truth—words and ideas that cut through appearances, through illusions like poverty, insufficiency, lack, and limitation.

Throughout this book, I suggest affirmations for you to use, and you will be encouraged to write your own.

Affirmations are most powerful when said aloud, while looking in a mirror. Look yourself in the eye. Say them with confidence and certainty—even if you don't believe a word of them!

Here are some powerful affirmations that are true in spirit. Believing them with *faith* will make them *true for you*!

- As I abundantly give, I abundantly receive. This is Divine Law.
- All my needs are met.
- My finances are constantly improving, and I am wealthy in many ways.
- My life is full of limitless possibilities for good.

---

[1] *Calvin and Hobbes* © 1995 Watterson. Reprinted with permission of Andrews McMeer Syndication. All rights reserved.

Prosperity Now! 9

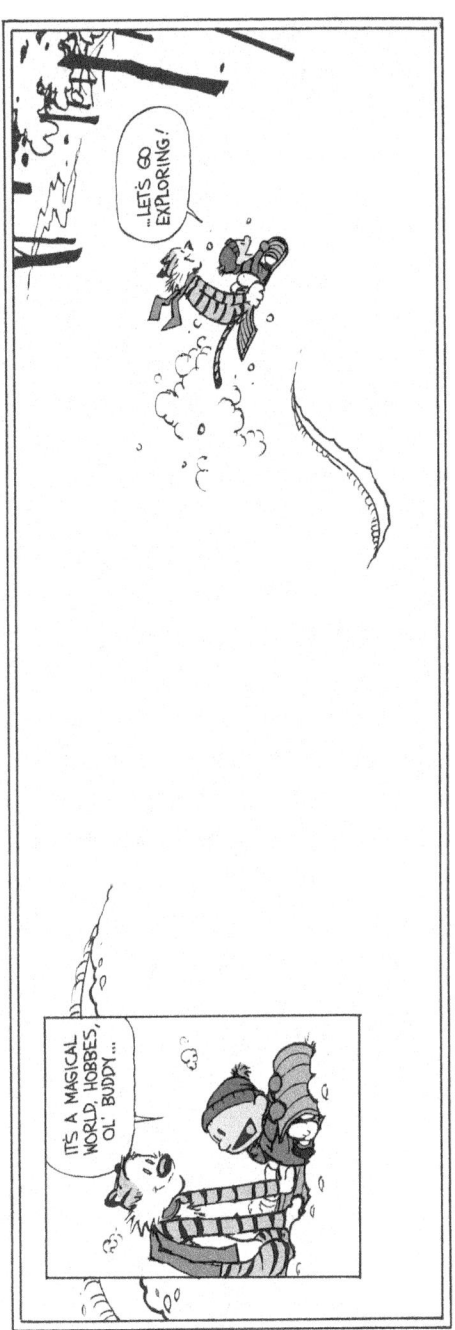

- There is a power for good in the universe greater than I am, and I can use it.
- I receive money abundantly and use money generously.

Select one of these affirmations, make it yours, and practice it at least twice a day. Write it down. Put it where you can see it—on a mirror or dresser. Let it sink into your subconscious and become part of your new thinking. It will become part of the new you.

Tithing

The concept of tithing comes from the Bible and from a farming culture. Civilization began with agrarian societies that settled down and grew crops instead of hunting and gathering. Many spiritual concepts are grounded in agricultural metaphors and examples.

A farmer stores away the harvest in a storehouse to survive the year. If the farmer sold or ate 100 percent of the grain, come spring, there would be nothing to plant for the next harvest. The farm would be ruined, and the family would starve.

So, good farmers save some seeds for planting, not eating. Even if they are hungry, they cannot eat the portion that has been set aside for next year's crop.

Really good farmers consciously select the best, fattest, healthiest seeds, knowing they will yield the best harvest next year.

In other words, the farmer sets aside the "first fruits" of the harvest to ensure an abundant, prosperous future.

The family lives on the remainder, in full faith they will have enough, and their increase is assured in the following season.

The amount generally set aside is a "tithe," or 10 percent of the harvest.

Tithe means 10 percent, or a tenth.

Spiritually, the concept of tithing is in the Book of Malachi in the Hebrew Bible, known as the Tanakh, or for Christians, the Old Testament:

> *"Bring your tithes into the storehouse, and test me now, and I will open the windows of heaven for you, and pour you out a blessing, that there shall not be room enough to receive it.."*
> — Malachi 3:10

We receive income, resources, and nourishment from various "fields." Whatever we receive at present is a good reflection of our prosperity consciousness. If we want to receive more, there are spiritual laws we can work with to increase our prosperity now.

Like the really good farmer, when our "crop" comes in (our paycheck, gifts, etc.), we take the "first fruits" and re-seed our spiritual field (consciousness) to reap a greater reward. We set aside a tenth of whatever we receive.

This is the tithe.

If we work for an employer and receive a regular check, we take 10 percent "off the top," before taxes are taken out.

If we are in business, self-employed, or an entrepreneur, we take our tithe *after* deducting necessary business expenses such as rent, utilities, supplies, etc. What is left over is our income, and we tithe from that.

Simple.

Where Should We Tithe?

This is also simple.

We tithe to the people and places where we get our spiritual nourishment—institutions, churches, authors, speakers, healing practitioners, etc. We tithe where we are fed spiritually, to whatever or whoever helps us to grow.

Wherever we get spiritual nourishment, that is where we tithe.

If you are using the Prosperity Now! course for self-study, then for the next twelve weeks, send your tithes to *Prosperity Now!* The address is on the website, prosperitynowlifeofdreams.com.

Remember, you made your contract with yourself and God. And you have my guarantee that, if you are unsatisfied, your tithes will cheerfully be refunded, after you complete the twelve weeks. Tithing to *Prosperity Now!* is a great way to get into the lifetime habit of tithing.

If your church or book study group is offering a *Prosperity Now!* group, tithe to your church during the class, not during the Sunday collection, so your tithes to *Prosperity Now!* can be tracked. Your church or study group should in turn tithe ten percent of the class tithes to Prosperity Now!

Remember—your satisfaction is guaranteed; your church will want to give you a full refund if you are not satisfied. Also, if you give cash, put it in an envelope with your name on it, again, so it can be tracked for the satisfaction guarantee.

It is important to note that tithing is not charity. You still can and should give to help the homeless, cure cancer, save the whales, etc. A tithe is like planting seeds, plowing back into the field of your consciousness ideas of abundance. Your tithe is a reinvestment in your spiritual consciousness— so it can grow deeper, broader, wider, fuller , which, in turn, will give you a deeper, richer, more fulfilling life.

Tithing should be prayerfully and thoughtfully done. Where are you being fed? Who is teaching you spiritual truths? What avenues has God brought you for spiritual growth? These places are where your tithes should go.

How to Tithe

In the beginning, I was an inconsistent tither, tithing sporadically. In my early, fitful tithing days, I noticed something.

When I tithed regularly, I would tithe with faith and assurance. I would be all right; my needs would be taken care of. I felt confident and connected to my Source. I felt ease in my mind, in my finances, and in my life.

When I stopped tithing, I became anxious about money and survival. I was more concerned, more hyper-vigilant about daily expenses. I was a penny-pincher. There was never enough....

When I did tithe, I noticed a strange thing happening...a clear miracle. It was a bit perplexing, but undeniable. Right there in black and white, in my checkbook register....

After tithing 10 percent, the remaining 90 percent stretched farther than the 100 percent used to!

When I had 100 percent of my money to spend, I was always short. There was never enough. When I tithed in faith to the Source of my spiritual nourishment, miraculously, the 90 percent covered all expenses—*and there was money left over*. This is a phenomenon illustrated in the biblical story of the loaves and fishes.

While Jesus is speaking, his disciples notice the crowd must be hungry. Let them leave so they can find food, they say. Jesus says, "No, *you* feed them." But they don't have enough (appearances)...only five loaves of bread and two fish (Matthew 14:17).

Jesus says to give him what they have. He blesses the bread and fish and tells the disciples to feed the crowd. Afterward, he says they should gather up the leftovers, which fill twelve baskets, much more than they started with.

This is a practical demonstration of the tithing instructions from Malachi. God specifically said, "Test me."

The small outlay of a mere 10 percent will elicit a response from the Universe that will boggle your mind. The outpouring of abundance—in all areas—that will come your way will be proof enough that tithing is a spiritual solution to a spiritual problem (weak faith, lack thinking, self-pity, fear, etc.) that plays out in physical reality (finances).

Tithe with confidence! Tithe with joy! If you feel fear while writing that tithe check, honor the illusion of fear. Feel it, but don't succumb to it. Put yourself in the hands of your Higher Power and watch the results!

One last word about how to tithe. Tithe from all sources.

We want to receive abundantly, and we have no idea what channels God will use to send us our good, so don't block the flow by limiting your tithing. Every channel of income is tithe-able.

I receive free massage certificates from a massage school I do work for that are worth $40 each, so I tithe $4.00. Once, I received a large insurance settlement of $86,000, so my tithe was $8,600. Believe me, the joy and gratitude I felt writing out anonymous $500, $1,000, and $2,000 checks to places that had supported me and fed me spiritually at that time cannot be described. You must feel that joy!

Did I gulp? Of course. Did a voice say, *"You idiot. You could do a lot with $8,600"*? You know it did and loudly, too. Very loudly. But my joy and faith were greater than my fear. My belief was in the abundance of the Universe, and I put it to the test. And....

It's a fact—my tithing today is vastly greater than my entire paycheck was when I started tithing.

Finally, tithing helps us remember something vital: There are lots of channels for good, but only one Source.

Thinking that our boss, our partner, our parents, or our job is the source of our income is a mistake, a dependence that sooner or later can and likely will let us down. All these channels are avenues for our good, but they are just channels for the One Source, the infinitely abundant Universe.

But I'm Too Poor to Tithe

This is a common, fear-based thought. But like all fear-based appearances, it has no basis in spiritual reality.

Saying "I'm too poor to tithe" is like saying, "I'm too stiff to do yoga." What an oxymoron. Yoga relieves stiffness. Tithing relieves financial "stiffness." If your current level of thinking is "I'm too poor. I'm struggling. I'm just getting by," then tithing is exactly what you need to do. It will wash away the fear and that erroneous thinking.

This program is all about healing our minds—our thinking—by taking action. We will learn to look past the fear, look past the appearance—the False Evidence Appearing Real (FEAR) to the truth in God, in Spirit.

Saying, "I'm too poor to tithe" is like saying, "I'm too hungry to eat." Think of tithing like feeding the soul, your soul, hungry and thirsty for a better life, new possibilities, new energy, fulfilling dreams beyond your wildest imagination.

No one can predict when, where, and how Spirit will respond to our small willingness, to our "mustard seed of faith," but truly it will respond, and only for our highest good.

In the Gospel of Matthew, there is a story of a boy "possessed by a demon." The father brings the boy to Jesus and says, "I brought him to your disciples, but they couldn't drive the demon out." Jesus heals the boy. Afterward, the disciples ask Jesus privately, "Why couldn't we cast out that demon?"

"You don't have enough faith," Jesus told them. "I tell you the truth, if you had faith even as small as a mustard seed, you could say to this mountain, 'Move from here to there,' and it would move. Nothing would be impossible."

The mustard seed is a metaphor for our faith journey because it is a very, very tiny seed, yet it grows to become a huge bush. Your tithing is like the mustard seed. It does not matter how large it is. After all, 10 percent of zero is—zero. Faith and willingness are what metaphorically move mountains.

Tithing feeds and nourishes our souls, changes our minds, and conforms our thinking to spiritual reality. Spiritual principles and laws that heal and uplift are food for our souls. We take one step toward our good and the Universe responds. It will respond by taking many steps toward our good.

How do we proceed? Well, we decide. Simple. Once you decide to change your mind, God will show you how.

Believe it. God will, without a doubt, show you how!

Goals and Goal Setting

A life with no goals is at best aimless, at worst, a dead-end path. True abundance and prosperity is a life filled with all the good the Universe can offer.

Earlier, in the "What Is Prosperity?" section, I listed some ideas about what prosperity might mean to you. Later, we'll talk more about setting goals in various areas of life. We will get some more insight into how to envision, energize, and manifest goals.

But to start, we need to focus narrowly—and consciously—on one goal. So....

Your Goal for the Course

Prayerfully, think of one goal you want to manifest during your twelve-week journey in Prosperity Now! Over the next twelve weeks, you will learn to focus on that goal powerfully, with joy and purpose. You will learn to "see it right" (i.e., seeing something that has not physically manifested yet), and ask the Universe to work with you to reach your goal.

An easy and fun way to "see it right" is to ask, "What would I do if money were no object?" Take money out of the equation and see where your heart's desire takes you.

Often, we can't hear our deepest longings. The noisy static of practicality drowns out our heart's yearnings, which otherwise would be strong and loud once we clear away the debris—something we will do in this journey together.

So, pick your one desire, your one goal for the course. Know it can be the foundation for future successes in all areas. As you grow in confidence and mastery, you will use these same ideas and tools and with greater skill.

When formulating your one goal, take fear of lack of money out of the equation. Then you will be better able to see your goal clearly and believe your goal is attainable.

Defining your goal without regard for money helps you see the first steps you need to take to move toward your goal. Failing (in your mind) before you even start is a common mistake. Taking the money question off the table lets you relax and begin to believe in possibilities.

What is the first step toward your goal? Your second step? The first step in the direction of your dream is usually simple and easily done. Maybe:

- Research it on the internet.
- Make a call.
- Ask advice from an expert or someone who is doing or has done what you want to do.
- Start a journal.
- Make an outline.
- Set a timeline.

All future actions will be easier, more practical, and hopeful when you ask, "What would I do if money was no object?"

Don't Ask "How?"

In conjunction with defining and taking steps toward your goal, it is important not to ask how something will be accomplished. This is a losing and distracting concern. How your goals are manifested is up to God. The Universe knows how. Surrender to that fact and move on. "What can I do today?" is the question, and it comes with setting your vision clearly and powerfully.

I once took Mary Morrissey's *Prosperity Plus* course and learned a phrase that works extremely well for me in goal setting and manifesting. It is perfectly tailored to "seeing it right."

The phrase is, "I am so happy and grateful now that [blank]." Fill in your stated goal, the goal you most desire, within your realm of believability.

When we cannot see something presently, that is where faith comes in. The power of this statement is that we state something in the present, as if it were in the past, while looking toward the future.

Let's restate that. You have a goal in mind. You activate your internal, mental, emotional, and spiritual energies by engaging the goal as if you have already achieved it!

This is the meaning behind Jesus' statement: "Therefore I tell you, whatever you ask in prayer, believe that you have received it, and it will be yours" (Mark 11:24).

Use Morrissey's statement, "I am so happy and grateful now that…," with your heartfelt goal in mind. It is a powerful way to visualize with faith.

ACTION ITEMS

Start a Prosperity Journal

This action is vital to your success. Start today putting down daily reflections. Write out your thoughts on the topics and answer the questions posed each week. Use this process to track your progress as you grow in consciousness.

Pick out a journal that says, "I am prosperous." A journal that reflects prosperity and abundance.

Start Saying Affirmations

1. Look yourself in the eye in a mirror and say, "I am prosperous" twenty-five times each day: morning, afternoon, and bedtime.
2. In addition, choose one of the affirmations from the list in this chapter and make it yours.
3. Recite both these affirmations while looking yourself in the eye.
4. Notice any resistance. This is vital to making any change—noticing the feelings and the blocks to our good, to the truth, and to change itself. Do you resist saying positive things about yourself?
5. What do you notice when you recite affirmations? What thoughts arise?

Answer these questions:

What is prosperity for me?

_____
_____
_____

What does prosperity look and feel like?

_____
_____
_____

Stretch yourself, beyond the limits of what you think you can believe. We will talk a lot about our beliefs, what they are, where they came from. We cannot achieve something we believe is impossible, silly, or grandiose, or that we believe we are not worthy of. Check your "believability limit" just to identify where it lies.

Reread Week 1 at Least Twice

I highly recommended you reread the lesson for the week at least twice. As you reread, jot down in your prosperity journal any ideas or questions you may have to discuss with others who are also doing *Prosperity Now!*

Take Step 1

Each week there is a step from twelve-step recovery, but modified to remove our old thinking about lack and limitation and instill ideas of prosperity and abundance.

By "taking a step," I mean read the step, meditate on the step, read literature about the step, talk with others who have taken the step, journal about what the step means to you and its implications for your life as it exists now, and how you would like it to be. Incorporate the steps into your life, for they will give you a new life!

Step 1 is "surrender." Surrender our old ideas, our old thoughts of lack, limitation, and unworthiness. Surrender any ideas of being undeserving. Surrender these negative ideas. Recognize how they make life unmanageable.

Pick a Twelve-Week Goal

Pick one goal, one desire you want to manifest in twelve weeks, one that makes your heart glad. Is it within your realm of believability? Write it down. It is your focus for the next twelve weeks.

Use Mary Morrissey's Phrase

"I am so happy and grateful now that [blank]" is powerful and it works! It sets up a vibration in our consciousness that "sees it right." It sees our goal as something already achieved.

The crux of spirituality and manifestation is knowing that God has our good already in hand, waiting for us to be ready to receive it. Keep this phrase for your heart's desire close at hand during your daily meditations and while doing your affirmations.

See your heart's desire as if it is already here, using faith to bring it to life.

Tithe[2]

Tithing is the heart of *Prosperity Now!* It will change your mind, lift up your eyes, and raise your consciousness out of the dense vibration of lack into the expansive sunlight of the Spirit.

When you tithe, feel the excitement and anticipation rising up. Feel the anticipation of good flowing to you. If you feel fear, pause and breathe. Fear will change to eagerness and enthusiasm with mindfulness and breathing.

When tithing, repeat your affirmation of abundance, and use this short prayer to bless your gifts:

> **Tithe**—*Divine Love, flowing through me, blesses and multiplies all that I have, all that I give, and all that I receive. We are blessed to know that Spirit is our Source. God bless! Thank you, God!*

Sing

"I Am So Blessed"[3]
by Karen Drucker

I Am so blessed
I Am so blessed
I Am so grateful, for all that I have
I Am so blessed, I Am so blessed
I Am so grateful, I Am so blessed

We are so blessed
We are so blessed
We are so grateful, for all that I have
We are so blessed, We are so blessed
We are so grateful, We are so blessed

Thank you, God!

To hear Karen Drucker's song, "I Am So Blessed" which accompanies each week's tithing, go to https://youtu.be/2SHaEjFtP2g.

---

2 Tithe income from all sources. If you are prepared to, begin to tithe today. If not, begin next week.
3 Reprinted with permission from KarenDrucker.com

Week 2
Change Your Thinking to Change Your Life

> *Prosperity is a way of living and thinking,*
> *and not just money or things.*
> *Poverty is a way of living and thinking,*
> *and not just a lack of money or things.*
> — Eric Butterworth, *In the Flow of Life*

Surrender

STEP 1 IS surrender, an admission that your thinking is old, tired, and ineffectual, and thus, you do things in old, tired, ineffectual ways—ways that stopped working long ago, if they ever worked at all.

By not fighting your old way of thinking and your old habits, by accepting who and where you are right now, and by surrendering to your reality in your consciousness and your daily life, you will be able to begin to break free.

Free to embrace new and better, more useful, and more *truthful* ideas.

Here is an affirmation that represents a new way to see yourself and the world:

> "I surrender to the innate wisdom of the Universe,
> which resides in me."

The Wisdom Within (God Within)

We are taught to look outside of ourselves for God—in the heavens or in the clouds. Think about it: Where does your attention go when you pray? When you think about your Higher Power, where do you immediately and unconsciously focus?

If you're like most people, you go outward, without even realizing or questioning it. But that is not where the Power of the Universe resides. God, the Universe, lies within us.

> *"I am in my Father, and you are in me,*
> *and I am in you."*
> — John 14:19-20

This seems complicated, but is really quite simple: We are a vital part of an infinite universe—the Universal One, whole and complete!

Engineers who design machines and systems plan them carefully and include every necessary part to make the system or machine work as designed. They never add extraneous parts.

Machines or systems designed by people do not have any unnecessary, extra parts, and the Universe is much more than a machine. It is a sublime system designed by an all-knowing, all-good Creator. As such, every part is vital and necessary, or the machine will not work as it should.

The Universe needs every individual part to function and be whole and perfect. Since you are in the Universe, you are a necessary part.

Take a moment to breathe that in. If you are here (and you are) then you are vital to the proper functioning of the Kingdom of God.

All Is One

The word "universe" has meaning and power: *"uni"* = *one*, *"verse"* = *version*.

The entire cosmos and *everything* in it is all one—a whole, indivisible piece.

Consider this: In the beginning, all was one substance: hydrogen, the simplest element known. As the gas contracted, gravity created great pressure and heat, pushing the hydrogen atoms into a dense mass. The molecular bonds were broken; the mass ignited to become a star.

The almost unimaginable heat created by burning hydrogen created helium, the second-most common element. And so on....

The other eighty-six natural elements were all created in this same way—in nuclear reactions inside stars and in huge stellar explosions known as supernovae.

That's right. Carbon (from which you are made), gold, lead, zinc, copper, uranium, etc. were all created in the furnaces of a trillion, trillion stars.

Every atom, every molecule in your body was once in the great engine of a star somewhere in the universe that exploded, spewing out its precious gift in every direction.

You are physically made of star stuff.

So, the quote from John 14—"I am in my Father (the Universe), and you are in me, and I am in you"—takes on new meaning.

The Truth Is: The Universe is literally in you, and you are literally in the Universe.

Thus, the Higher Power/Wisdom of God—aka Christ or God Consciousness, Buddha Consciousness, Krishna Consciousness, or the Higher Self is in you.

It is available to you. It is always working for your greatest good.

Rather than relying on habitual thinking, which doesn't yield very good results, we practice surrendering to the wisdom, the power within us, which is available 24/7. This inner wisdom actually knows the complete picture.

The Wisdom of God knows what we need to say, to do, and to *be* to have abundance, serenity, and a full life.

> "But when they hand you over, do not worry about how to respond or what to say. In that hour, you will be given what to say. For it will not be you speaking, but the Spirit of God speaking through you."
> — Matthew 10:19-20:

Surrendering, relaxing into the assurance that we have an unlimited inner resource to guide and direct us, should be very comforting.

Modern society has become reliant upon the internet. All sorts of information and resources are available with just a few keystrokes or mouse clicks. We take it so much for granted that when we accidentally forget our devices, we are lost. We can't find a restaurant, settle a bar bet, look up a word, or keep up with the latest news.

Yet, for eons, humankind has had an inner guide and all-knowing resource within, ready, willing, and able—eager—to help us. We just need to listen!

Tuning into this innate wisdom takes some practice and perseverance, but it is a sure bet. Information on the internet may be wrong, but God's guidance is surefire.

My good friend Reverend Jon Mundy, writer and mystic, *A Course in Miracles* teacher, and director of the All-Faiths Seminary International in New York City, where I was ordained as an interfaith minister, is fond of saying that we have a God-given GPS system that we can learn to use. Unerring and always pointing toward our good, this spiritual GPS is *"God's Plan for Salvation."*

God's plan for salvation (GPS) can and will guide us unceasingly, certainly, gently, and lovingly toward our highest good, toward our heart's desires, toward what we deserve as beloved Children of God.

We need to be in tune with our innate wisdom to enjoy a full and rich life. It will show us the way to mastery, if we let it, through consistent perseverance and practice.

Getting aligned in the direction of our heart's desires and our highest good means consciously stating, to the best of our present ability, who we are and where we would like to be in the future.

For this we will need a Mission, a Vision, and a Motto.

Mission, Vision, and Motto

Since you are clearly a vital part of the Universe—of God's plan—you ought to have guidance and direction. You have a mission. It is important to clarify your mission and to set a vision for yourself, for your life-direction.

As someone once said, "If we don't change where we're going, we'll end up where we're headed." If we have been living an aimless, purposeless life, with no clear direction, no clear goals or vision, we will likely end up somewhere we don't want to be.

Going from New York to San Francisco without a map, compass, or plan, we might arrive there eventually by random chance, but we're more likely to end up somewhere else and no telling what that place will be like.

Over the next few weeks, one *Prosperity Now!* action step will be to write a mission statement, a vision statement, and a motto for life. These are not detailed and specific statements. They are broad, overarching themes that set a direction.

What is the difference between mission and vision? Britt Skrebanek, co-owner and principal consultant at Superneat Marketing, defines them this way:

> A mission statement focuses on today and what an organization (or a person) does to achieve [its mission].
>
> A vision statement focuses on tomorrow and what an organization (or person) wants to ultimately become.
>
> Both are vital in directing goals.

All major enterprises have mission and vision statements. They give a company a solid foundation (a mission) for today and guiding principles (vision) to work toward.

Take Facebook, for example. Here are its mission and vision:

Mission: To give people the power to build community and bring the world closer together.

Vision: People use Facebook to stay connected with friends and family, to discover what's going on in the world, and to share and express what matters to them.

Another excellent example is Southwest Airlines.

Mission: The mission of Southwest Airlines is dedication to the highest quality of customer service delivered with a sense of warmth, friendliness, individual pride, and company spirit.

Vision: To become the world's most loved, most flown, and most profitable airline.

Notice neither says much about making money or becoming a behemoth multi-national company. Success in all areas comes naturally when we are true to our highest good and our intuition, and when we surrender our old thinking to the innate wisdom that resides inside us.

GoDaddy, the internet web-hosting and domain name company, has a fun, powerful mission statement and a truly visionary vision statement.

Mission: We are here to help our customers kick ass. We do that by living our strategy and ruthlessly prioritizing our work to create simple, elegant technology that delights our customers—all while delivering service that is second to none. Every single day, we join forces across teams and groups to break down barriers, build new markets, and stare down the impossible until the impossible blinks.

Vision: We will radically shift the global economy toward small business by empowering people to easily start, confidently grow, and successfully run their own ventures.

Knowing who you are today (mission) and knowing where you want to be headed (vision) are vital to success. The clearer these are, the better your chances for success.

Both statements ought to be reviewed and updated from time-to-time so they stay fresh and in line with our current beliefs, our recent growth or changing goals, and our freshest, newest, most up-to-date spiritual understanding.

Personal Statements

I recently revised my personal mission statement, which reflects my guiding principles for my life and for my work teaching people spiritual principles of prosperity and healing from physical illness. Here are my mission and vision statements:

My mission: To teach and to heal, using spiritual truths as I grow in understanding and love. I am a joyful example of the power of Spirit to overcome all obstacles.

My vision: I bring inspiration, hope, and peace of mind to all who seek it, and I bring compassion and patience to those who suffer. I grow in joy, understanding, and love.

These statements give me a solid base on which to build and clear direction in which to move. I refer to them frequently and measure what I am doing, saying, planning, believing, and espousing based on their direction and guidance.

Once our mission and vision statements are in place, we can begin to structure a life and a series of life goals that meet these mission and vision statements.

Motto

A motto is a short phrase or a word, a "bumper sticker" for your life. It is not specific, like "Get a car!" It is a broad, directional, sharp, short, and snappy idea that acts like a compass for every specific thing you want to be and have and do. An excellent company motto relates to the enterprise's mission and vision and is catchy and memorable.

Disney's "The happiest place on earth" let's you know what the organization is all about. It clearly states what the company strives for and wants to be for its customers. It is evident how the employees see themselves and what motivates their every move and decision.

Nokia, the phone and telecommunications giant, has a motto that is about as simple as one could be, and yet it is powerful, describing what they strive to do: "Connecting people." Simple. Elegant. They picked this motto at the start of the mobile phone era, when there was no easy way for people to connect, and they have never changed it.

Apple's "Think Different" came at a time when the company was failing. PCs were dominating and competitors were being squeezed out. Steve Jobs positioned the company as revolutionary and anti-establishment. He was saying, "You're different. We're different. We're a counterculture, worlds away from the stuffy business suit-and-tie computers that older people use. We offer possibilities they'll never think of. Join Throw us. Think different."

A good motto can drive your energies, and the energy of the people around you, in quiet but powerful ways. My motto is simple, and in French, which helps me with my lifetime goal of living in France. It was formulated quite a few years ago. I've seen no need to change it since. It is: *Vivez joyeux!* It means simply, *"Live happily!"* or *"Live joyously!"*

When I remember my motto, I am called to think about what I'm doing, how I'm feeling and thinking, and how I'm acting and reacting in everyday situations. My motto keeps me on track. It keeps me from becoming sidetracked, distracted, and off-balance.

Create a motto for yourself—for the life you want to have, for the person you want to be, every day in every situation. Create a motto for yourself that encapsulates your mission and vision, your dreams, your meta-goal for life.

Your Goal

Last week, you were asked to come up with a goal to accomplish by the end of our twelve weeks. I hope you have done that.

Once you have mission, vision, and motto in place, over the coming weeks, look again at the goal you set. Is your stated goal in line with the mission, vision, and motto you laid out? Do they all line up?

You might want to review or revise your goal in the light of your mission and vision statements. Or vice versa. Do not be afraid to change your mind in the face of new information or new insight.

Your mission and vision statements will change and evolve over time. Your motto may be replaced by something that reflects the new you, which comes about as the result of your new thinking.

Your specific goal for the course is not a fixed, immovable thing. It can be tweaked to make it something that suits you better, so now is the time to line everything up. Put everything "in alignment" because that is a powerful way to achieve success. Everyone is rowing in the same direction—head, heart, hands, guts, feet, intention—all in perfect alignment.

Remember: We cannot be internally aligned if we have ideas that run counter to the truth of Spirit and the spiritual laws we are beginning to learn and work with. Old, stale ideas weigh us down and push us off course. Over the coming weeks, we will eliminate and shift these old ideas to make room for newer, truer ones.

Sharing Your Goal

To generate energy, to help manifest your goal, first in your mind and then in physical reality, share your goal with like-minded people. People who share your enthusiasm for your vision can be great "booster rockets." They reinforce your belief, hold your vision for you, and envision your dream with you. I call the people in my inner circle my "Spiritual Board of Directors." They are the ones I can call on to be supportive sounding boards, give advice, or just listen.

The power of "two or more" gathered together with like-mindedness to envision a plan or a goal cannot be understated. Energies and forces multiply when people focus with intention. A team of supporters, cheerleaders, and encouraging people is necessary to any endeavor. This is the phenomenon of the power of the GPS increased exponentially!

> *"Again, I tell you, if two of you agree about anything you ask for, it will be done for you by God in heaven. For where two or three gather together in My name (in my Way), I am there with them."*
> — Matthew 18:19-20

Sometimes your support team will see further than you can alone. They will give encouragement and support you when your belief falters. People can often believe for us what we cannot believe for ourselves. They see our progress when we cannot. They can be more objective, being detached emotionally from a situation.

However, we must choose wisely with whom we share our goals and dreams. Those who give energy, validate, support, and have our best interests at heart are safe to confide in. Their energy will magnify and expand our vision and our enthusiasm. They can add extra juice to our goal.

Yet there are those people—sometimes those closest to us—who can dampen our enthusiasm. Even if they mean well, they can throw cold water onto our cherished hopes and dreams. Those who are cynical, suffering from their own "poverty consciousness," jealous, negative, or otherwise lacking in vision can dampen our energy and enthusiasm and stifle our dreams.

You must be careful not to "cast your pearls before swine." This biblical metaphor means, "Do not drop your treasure among those who will not, who cannot, understand, lest they turn and trample your vision."

With these people, it is best to say nothing. They are acting unconsciously out of their own mistaken beliefs, and they get what they are looking for.

Also, it is sound wisdom to keep your dream-energy well-contained in a focused psychic space. Bragging, talking loosely, leaking information to people unable to hear it, dissipates and dilutes your vision's vibrancy. It can be unwise and even destructive to your plans.

Share selectively. Hold your cards close to your vest. Disclose your vision only to those who will support it, adding energy, enthusiasm, and zeal to you and your cherished dream. Their support will boost your belief, and these allies are invaluable resources.

Then, when you manifest your goal, when your light shines brightly for all to see, when people who were not paying the slightest attention suddenly are aware that something has obviously changed in you, people will question, "What happened? What does she have? What's different? I can't put my finger on it, but something…."

Steven Mitchell, in his extremely popular translation of the *Tao Te Ching*, Poem 17 writes:

> *The Master doesn't talk, he acts.*
> *When his work is done,*
> *the people say, "Amazing:*
> *we did it, all by ourselves!"*

People will see the results but not the changes and hard work. They will ascribe your prosperity to luck, good fortune, or wealthy relatives. Those who are ready may be curious enough to ask and start to follow the path you have opened up for them.

Share your goals judiciously. Gather a spiritual board of directors around you. Engage the powerful energies created by gathering "two or three together."

Affirmations

Last week, we spoke about affirmations, positive prayer that aligns our thinking with reality, spiritual reality—ultimate reality. Affirmations are fun. People like to use and say them.

But something must come before the affirmation to push out the old, the "false evidence appearing real" (FEAR), and make room for the affirmation. We need….

Denials

Denials, used in conjunction with affirmations, clear a path to bring our thinking into alignment with the truth.

Denials must come first to clear out our mental, emotional, and spiritual psychic space—which needs to be emptied of our old, tired, worthless, useless, ineffective, weak, and false ideas—so new fresh, alive, vital, affirming, and joyous ideas can come into our consciousness.

You can't make a cluttered, dirty room useful until you clean it out. Throwing out garbage, fixing what's broken, and making it ready is a precursor to having a bright, clean, useable space.

You can't have a nice, healthy, prosperous garden on land that is full of debris, weeds, shrubs, and poor soil. You must clear out all the old brush and get the soil nice and healthy before anything will grow.

It is the same with our minds, our thinking, and our consciousness. We can't put new, fresh ideas in a mind that's cluttered with negative, false, and useless information. We must pull out the old stuff before the new, positive, useful ideas will take root.

Therefore, journaling is important. Journaling moves our thoughts out to where they can be examined and, if necessary, released. We let go; we declutter.

Denials do that. Denial statements clear out the lies, untruths, and misinformation we may have learned as children, in the media, or through other sources.

Denials create a vacuum that we must fill with positive thoughts and feelings. It is vital that we follow up a denial with an affirmation.

Examples of denials include:

- There is no lack of substance, of life, or intelligence anywhere.
- Lack, poverty, fear, and want cannot rule me. I know they are not real.
- There is nothing for me to fear.
- The thought of lack has no power over me.
- There is no scarcity in the Universe.
- I am not limited by any appearances.
- Loss and insufficiency do not exist in Spirit and in Truth.

Pick one of these denial statements and put it before the positive affirmation you selected last week. Denials go before an affirmation. Write both out and put them in places where you will see them often.

Denials and affirmations work well when you say them aloud, consciously, in front of a mirror. But they also work on a subconscious level when you walk by them and don't consciously notice them. Your subconscious notices them!

Denials are the jackhammers that will break up the hardened soil, the old ideas that have hardened like concrete. Denials are powerful. They wear away fixed and static ideas, pulverizing them to be washed away in the clear flow of our affirmations.

Resistance

It's understandable that resistance and doubt will arise when you're working to release the past and raise your level of consciousness. Old, fixed thoughts carry a lot of baggage. After all, they were given to you by people you loved. People generally have a lot invested in being right—or at least their egos do. Old ideas often do not go away quietly or lightly.

This won't work. I can't change. This is hard. It may work for others, but not for me. This kind of thinking is natural because our old consciousness is our comfort zone, and we are being asked to step way past the edge of our comfort zone.

Charles Fillmore, co-founder of the Unity Movement, had a name for this process of introducing new Truth ideas, followed by resistance. He called it "chemicalization." The old ideas resist being eradicated. It is the "adjustment period" when we are acclimating to the new ideas, while feeling the pull of the old ideas and behaviors. Changing a lifetime's way of thinking is not always easy!

These sprouts of resistance and doubt need to be pulled up like weeds in a garden that chokes off the new plants—the fragile ideas (seedlings) that are just taking root. When you don't see immediate results, or you fail to quickly lose your fear or anger, do not be discouraged. Fillmore reminds us that the spiritual ideas are more powerful than the ego-based fears.

Do not despair. Relax! Let go! Do your first step surrender and trust the process. Breathe slowly and use first your denial followed by your affirmation. To overcome resistance, notice it and relax with a slow, deep breath. Breathing is a powerful tool to decrease anxiety, fear, and doubt and increase trust, serenity, and acceptance.

"Not my will, but Thine be done."

Step 2—Came to believe that a power greater than ourselves could restore us to sanity.

When a person does something repeatedly, something that doesn't work or causes pain, something is seriously wrong with their thinking. They may long for a new way of life, yet days, weeks, months, and years pass and things stay the same—or get worse for them. Not a clinical definition of insanity, but not evidence of mental—or spiritual—health either.

Restoring sanity for *Prosperity Now!* means you are ready to give up old ideas, ideas that don't work anymore—if they ever did work, replacing them with fresh, new ideas, invigorated with power and life.

The word "restore" implies that we were once sane and we always have been in Spirit. Once upon a time, we probably had saner, more accurate ideas about life, God, money, relationships, etc. But that healthy thinking was eroded away by what we learned over the years.

However it happened, our lives have not panned out how we hoped. Or maybe we have success in certain areas, but others are lacking. Either way, we need to significantly change our thinking to live the full life of our dreams.

Step 2 clearly states that *we* do not change our thinking, at least not alone. It is clear that a Higher Power, one greater than us, will bring us back to sanity and higher-order thinking. This is a wonderful and encouraging promise. We have an ally, ready, willing, and able to work with us and for us. God will do the heavy lifting when we are willing to do our part in the process.

Also, clearly "coming to believe" is not an event, but a process. Take it as a promise. If we are willing to head in a new direction, we can live "happy, joyous, and free."

After all, if we do not believe we can have a life of our dreams, the alternative is we will be stuck forever. Being open-minded and surrendering to the idea that God can and will restore our right-mindedness is what Step 2 is all about.

If we do our best and persist, we will soon see evidence that we are being restored. New thoughts will pop up, and we will recognize they did not come from our old thinking and old beliefs.

I once was in tremendous emotional pain and went into the shower to wash, but also to cry. Showers are great places to feel emotions because, metaphysically, emotions are represented by water. I was having a good hard cry when a clear voice said to me, "This pain will end." I stopped in an instant, realizing this was not a "John thought!" It clearly came from a new place in my consciousness, in my spirit. It was the part of me that is eternal and has always been fully awake and in touch with God. And I was waking up to it.

Believe that this can and will happen for you. You will soon enough see the glimmers of new light in the darkness. It is a virtual guarantee.

The use of a denial followed by an affirmation is a powerful vehicle on the road to being restored to sanity, literally aligning our consciousness with the Mind of the Universe.

Believe this is possible. Believe it is possible for you. Believe you are doing it...because you are!

ACTION ITEMS
Start Saying Denials

Denials must come before affirmations. Choose one of the denial statements listed above. Write it down. Denials break up the hardened concrete of these old ideas. Often, they are not fun. Reciting denials and affirmations can seem like drudgery. This is to be expected. If you were jackhammering a sidewalk, it would be hard, dusty, and strenuous work. It may take a while before you see any measurable results.

Continue Saying Affirmations

Continue reciting your two affirmations—"I am prosperous" and the affirmation you picked last week—in a mirror to yourself twenty-five times, three times per day.

Speak the truth to your conscious and subconscious minds. Affirmations fill the vacuum left behind when you deny old ideas that are not true. Write them down in your journal and on notes around the house, in your car, etc. Your subconscious mind will see them, even when you don't notice them consciously. Hearing them aloud in your own voice, in your own ears, retrains your mind to think in terms of truth—God's Truth!

Begin to Work With a Surrender Statement

Now we will add a third statement of truth to recite in addition to our denial and affirmation: *I surrender to the innate wisdom of the Universe that resides in me.*

Feel the surrender. Notice any resistance: tight shoulders, strained eyes, furrowed forehead, clenched hands, wherever you hold tension. What are you guarding against, exactly? Remember, "chemicalization," the transition period when the old ideas are resisting being released. Rest assured, the spiritual truths you are learning are more powerful and will soon be yours.

Relax and ease into the certainty that a loving Higher Power wants the best for you and knows what you need to do to get it. We are not giving up (surrendering) anything of value, anything good or lasting. We are giving up ego-control, which is an illusion. Putting our minds, hearts, and thoughts on God first, we embark on a new way of living that has proven, positive results—results that work and are enduring.

Practice Noticing

Where does your attention go? When you think of God, the Universe, your Higher Power, or Spirit, notice where your attention goes. Inward or outward? If it is going outside, begin gently redirecting your attention inside.

Noticing, aka awareness, is what we are after in *Prosperity Now!* This is more than half the battle. Once we notice something, we can begin to examine it and change it. If we don't know we have a problem, we will never seek a solution. Noticing where our attention goes when we pray allows us to set in our mind exactly where the power of the Universe resides—inside of you!

Create Your Mission Statement

What are you? Who are you? Your mission statement puts the focus on today. This is a good opportunity to practice surrender. Don't write your mission statement alone. Ask God what your mission is and surrender. Listen for the answer. The words will come, and you will feel when it is right.

This is not necessarily an easy action item. Don't be discouraged if the perfect mission statement doesn't flow from your pen in one go. It will likely take several drafts, edits, and rewrites to get something that resonates with your soul. Patience and persistence will pay off.

Next week, we will focus on the Vision Statement.

Reread Week 2 at Least Twice

> ***Tithe***—*Divine Love, flowing through me, blesses and multiplies all that I have, all that I give and all that I receive. We are blessed to know that Spirit is our Source. God bless! Thank you, God!*

Sing

"I Am So Blessed"
by Karen Drucker

I Am so blessed
I Am so blessed
I Am so grateful, for all that I have
I Am so blessed, I Am so blessed
I Am so grateful, I Am so blessed

We are so blessed
We are so blessed
We are so grateful, for all that we have
We are so blessed, We are so blessed
We are so grateful, We are so blessed

Thank You, God!

Week 3
Happy, Joyous, and Free!

Moses said to God, "When they ask who sent you?
What is His name? What do I tell them?"
God said, "I am who I am.
Tell the children of Israel, 'I Am sent me.'"
— Exodus 31:13-14

Take the Easy Way!

MAYBE YOU HAVE worked hard, struggled, fought, and persevered when you wanted to quit. Maybe you thought you were getting ahead, only to slide backwards due to some "random" bad luck: the car broke down, you got laid off from work, or a health issue sapped your meager savings.

A struggle, a setback, a fight, "keeping my head above water," etc. are all images of the way the world sees life's journey—drudgery, a slog, a treadmill.

Learning and practicing spiritual principles in *Prosperity Now!*, we begin to lighten the load, working *with* the flow, instead of struggling against it.

Someone once said, "Don't mistake motion for progress." What a great reminder. Like a car spinning its wheels in sand, a lot of energy is being expended with noise, smoke, and mostly wasted effort. And the car has not gone anywhere.

Shifting from self-reliance and determination to ease and freedom is the subject of Jesus' words in Matthew 11:28-30:

> *"Come to me, all you who are weary
> and burdened, and I will give you rest.
> Take my yoke upon you and learn from me,
> for I am gentle and humble in heart,
> and you will find rest for your souls.
> For my yoke is easy and my burden is light."*

Working unnecessarily hard, relying solely on our own efforts, and mentally fighting uphill against the world is a tiring and heavy way to live. Daily living by spiritual law is liberating.

Living this way is simple, but not easy for the ego: we must humble ourselves. The easier softer way is to acknowledge that we *are* dependent on God. To achieve any real prosperity, any lasting peace of mind, we must begin to trust and rely upon the higher laws of the Universe. They work.

This is the way to freedom, not enslavement; to ease, not drudgery; to hope, not despair.

We will talk more about this in upcoming weeks but for now, know that you can be certain this wisdom, this guidance, this energy of God is available. It will work in you—and through you. It is the easy way!

What's in a Name?

Keep in mind, when Jesus said, "I" and "my," he didn't mean himself as a human man. He was not speaking personally. He was referring to the power of God within him, which is also within you.

Jesus is an example—a teacher—of what anyone can do when they are completely connected to God. He speaks and acts directly from that consciousness in every one of us—the aspect of God in you, that is you.

Call it Christ Consciousness, Buddha Mind, the Innate Wisdom of the Universe, God Consciousness, Krishna Consciousness, Intuition, or whatever you like.... It's all the same.

Maybe you have heard someone say, "In Jesus' name," as if the name Jesus is a magical incantation. They may think, "If I say this name loudly enough or long enough, my life will change."

A Course in Miracles states, "The Bible says, "Ask in the name of Jesus Christ." Is this merely an appeal to magic? A name does not heal… What does calling on his name confer? (*A Course in Miracles: Manual for Teachers*, Chapter 22)

"What does this mean to you? It means that in remembering Jesus, you are remembering God."

The books of the Bible, the Old and New Testaments, came from cultures where the English word "name" is more accurately translated as "way."

They were saying, "In Jesus' way," or in other words, asking what we believe Jesus would say or do in our situation.

I once heard my good friend, Reverend Jim Fuller, give a sermon on this topic. He pointed out that if you wanted to split an atom, you wouldn't say the name Einstein over and over. You would do it in the way Einstein demonstrated.

If you want spiritual prosperity and abundance, you do it in the way spiritual masters have demonstrated.

The Flow of the Tao (Dao)

The name of the ancient Chinese spiritual text, the *Tao Te Ching*, can be translated as "The Book of the Way (or Path)."

Taoism is a deep and profound expression of the natural flow of the Universe. A person who discerns the Way of the Universe, the Tao of the Universe, will flow in harmony with the Laws of the Universe and with all Life.

These natural, spiritual laws can be discerned, learned, applied, and practiced with greater skill and mastery. They can be used throughout life to be in accord with the times, with how lifeworks and the way things are, with the flow of *chi*, or life-energy.

By aligning our minds with the Way of the Universe, we have a powerful friend and ally who can "*[do] for us what we cannot do for ourselves.*" (*The Big Book*)

My favorite translation of the *Tao Te Ching* is by Stephen Mitchell. It has been used by millions to acquaint themselves with this nearly 2,500-year-old text that is the basis for much of Buddhism, Zen Buddhism, and Confucianism. The *Tao Te Ching* is also the foundation for the I Ching, Chi Gong, Aikido, the other martial arts, and the Eastern arts of poetry, painting, gardening, calligraphy, and flower arranging.

Tao is about many things, but it is above all about the movement, the flow of the Universe, of the Tao. It attempts to explain in words what is inexplicable. We cannot see the Tao, but we can see its effects.

Mitchell's version of Poem 15 starts:

> *The ancient Masters were profound and subtle.*
> *Their wisdom was unfathomable.*
> *There is no way to describe it;*
> *All we can describe is their appearance.*
> *They were careful*
> *as someone crossing an iced-over stream.*
> *Alert as a warrior in enemy territory.*
> *Courteous as a guest.*
> *Fluid as melting ice.*
> *Shapeable as a block of wood.*
> *Receptive as a valley.*
> *Clear as a glass of water.*

To be like these masters is not only possible; it is the easy way. If we harness the benevolent powers available to us, we will be ready for anything and ready to turn anything to our advantage.

Setbacks become new and better pathways.

Obstacles become opportunities.

Stumbling blocks become steppingstones.

The Way of the Tao is best described as yielding and returning. We yield to the flow and let it direct our steps. We return to the Source, receiving nourishing ideas and peaceful rest and submitting to the will of our Higher Power.

That Power will help us; it is always there the same way electric current is always available, always there, silent but ready to bring us our greatest good, bring us everything we need and desire, everything that is in alignment with our Highest and Best Good.

I Am = God's Name (God's Way)

God said, "I am who I am. Tell the children of Israel, 'I Am sent me."

Referring to the quote at the start of today's reading, the Name (the Way) of the Power of the Universe is I Am.

When we say, "I am [blank]," everything that follows declares to the Universe what we think, believe, know, understand, and expect. And the Universe responds perfectly!

Saying or thinking, "I am [blank]," sets up a vibration—in ourselves, in our subconscious minds, and in the Universe. And the Universe responds at the same vibrational frequency.

We create our world, our circumstances, and our lives, by our thoughts, beliefs, and words.

When someone asks, "How are you?" what is your standard response? "I'm okay," "I'm fine," "I'm so-so," or just, "Meh"?

These bland replies, used thoughtlessly, declare to the Universe what our current state of mind is—and how we expect life to be.

What you *think* and *say* is what you get. Energy flows exactly to where our attention goes.

If, however, we declare with enthusiasm, "I am prosperous!" what are we saying? How does that statement feel? How does it resonate in our minds and hearts, in our bones, and in the very air around us?

Feel the excitement. Feel the joy. Feel the possibilities by declaring your new truth and expressing your confidence in your new reality. Watch carefully; notice what you say and how you feel. Whenever you say, "I am," if it is not a declaration of the highest, positive good, change it immediately.

Tithing— "Seek First the Kingdom"

In Week 1, I said tithing is a well-tested concept that frees our minds from ideas of lack, scarcity, and poverty. The action of tithing moves us from feelings of "not enough," waking us up to the Universe's infinite abundance.

We talked about how a *really smart* farmer sets aside the first fruits and the best seeds of the harvest so the following year's yield will be bigger and better.

Money is not a bad thing. It's just spiritual energy, like everything else. But because of the heavy baggage most people put on money, it is a great vehicle we can use to break up old thinking, sow new spiritual seeds, and grow our spiritual consciousness of abundance.

We create thoughts of greater prosperity and abundance by taking action. Then our new, expanded consciousness will show up in our outer reality—in our lives.

In the activity of tithing, we are changing our perspective and our priorities. Tithing from the "first fruits" demonstrates to the Universe that we are putting God first!

This new perspective is 180 degrees away from how the world thinks. Worldly thinking says, "I must pay all my obligations right away. Oh! and then I'll tithe.... If there is anything left over." That thinking puts the world first.

Tithing *first* tells the Universe our priorities and perspectives have shifted. We demonstrate that we are, "seeking first the Kingdom of God." In Matthew 6, Jesus tells the crowd, "Do not worry about what you will eat or drink or wear. Your Father in Heaven knows you need these things. But seek you first the Kingdom of Heaven, and His righteousness and all these things will be added unto you."

Seek first the Kingdom, and know that all your needs will be met! That is pointing faith in the right direction, away from misguided faith in worry and insufficiency.

We are righting our topsy-turvy ideas about how God works, and in the bargain, we have a pretty good guarantee from God, who says to test this theory out for yourself. We are actually invited to test the Universe and see what happens.

The Truth Is: God does not need money, but you need to be free.

The action of tithing takes courage (at first). It will eliminate old, fear-based thinking. It will wash away those ineffective and false ideas that keep you stuck at your present level of consciousness.

You need to be liberated from old consciousness so you can soar to new levels of freedom and abundance.

As I told you, my tithe check today is much larger than my entire paycheck was when I started tithing. And more importantly, all areas of my life have increased. My health is infinitely better than it was back then, my friendships have grown and deepened, my experiences have been rich and meaningful, and even the difficulties have proven to be blessings.

And most of all, my peace of mind, serenity, and trust that my Higher Power will work on my behalf has grown tremendously!

But because money means survival to most people, the concept of tithing can go to the very core of our fears, our worries, our beliefs about money and all that it implies: status, advancement, nourishment, medical care, transportation, leisure, housing, etc.

A common reaction is: "What? My bills are more than my income. If I tithe, I must live on 90 percent? It can't be done." This response is understandable, but 180 degrees opposed to the way spiritual law works.

Remember: This course is not about how to make more money. It is about expanding and opening our minds—moving from small, meager thinking to vast, enlivening, and abundant thinking.

Ten percent may seem too big of a pill to swallow, but just try it for these twelve weeks. See how it feels. See what reactions and resistance come up, but also, notice the feelings of freedom, of courage, of possibility that will definitely arise. Tithe the full 10 percent and don't look back!

Ten percent is not a magic number, but it has proven successful for millions upon millions of people for centuries and centuries. And there are those who tithe more. There are stories of people who tithe 90 percent and live on 10 percent. Sound farfetched? Well, consider your present circumstances. If tomorrow you made $10 million, couldn't you give away $9 million and live on $1 million?

As we said in Week 1, a tithe is not charity. It is an investment in our spiritual growth and, therefore, it goes to the places, people, or institutions from which we receive our spiritual nourishment. Yes, give to the Red Cross, the animal shelter, or whatever you want to support. But a tithe is different. It's an investment in you and your future.

As a functional matter, the Universe has unlimited avenues of flowing good to you. By tithing from all sources, we don't choke off the supply.

And always, always, tithe with joy and gratitude, never with overwhelming fear. There may be a little fear, so stop and examine that feeling.

Fear is appropriate...if there's a tiger charging at you. Otherwise, it may be something else. Conscious, deep breathing can turn fear into excitement.

If you feel fear, stop. Relax. Go into a quiet, listening state. Notice how you feel. Notice any resistance. Slow and deepen your breath and your mind to really notice there is joy and a sense of possibility ready to spring forth once you move past any fear.

Watch and see the fear dissipate and change to excitement and anticipation. A healthy, loving, powerful part of you that has been in the background is being moved up into your awareness. That part knows you are worthy of receiving more and more and more.

Give your tithe cheerfully. Give it with joy. Give it with love. Give it in anticipation of your highest good returning to you tenfold—a hundredfold!

And so, it is.

Hope and Faith

Hope and faith are distinctly different. Hope is expecting our good in the future that hasn't arrived yet. Faith is knowing our good is already here. It has arrived, but we don't see it. If we could see it, we wouldn't need faith. We only need faith when we cannot see with our physical eyes. We may not yet have spiritual "eyes to see and ears to hear," but we will develop them, beyond physical sight.

Just as faith is needed only in the absence of something, courage only arises when fear is perceived. No fear, no need for courage.

I believe that when we overcome something that scares us, we get courage as a reward, courage that will come in handy in the next scary situation. Courage and faith work together to help us overcome obstacles and move forward.

> *"Now faith is the substance of things hoped for, the evidence of things not seen."*
> — Hebrews 11:1

If we have faith, we don't need physical proof. Our faith is the proof. If we can see our new car, we don't need faith to see it sitting outside. Faith, the "evidence," only arises when there is not yet physical evidence of something.

The great French mathematician, inventor, and philosopher Blaise Pascal once said, "The heart has its reasons of which reason knows nothing." Faith is not logical; it is often counterintuitive. It makes no sense and appears to the world as foolishness, Pollyanna-like naïveté, or even stupidity. Yet faith is a solid, substantial attribute.

The Truth Is: We have faith, and we use that faith all of the time.

However, people think they don't have enough faith, or that they lack faith, or that they have lost faith.

The Truth Is: You cannot lose faith. You cannot acquire more faith.

The Truth Is: You have, right now, within you, all the faith you will ever need.

The Great Spirit, the Innate Wisdom of the Universe, is within us. We have infinite faith within us. Our faith is always active, so the real question is: Are we in touch with our faith and in which direction is it going?

Likely, our faith has been unconsciously activated in the wrong direction. We might unconsciously have faith in "Murphy's Law." We might have faith that we are unworthy, that we're not bright, or that we are unlucky or sad all the time, or that we are the sick one in our family, or we are the "rebellious one," or that we [fill in the blank].

Notice the old, tired, useless, false messages we tell ourselves that were probably told to us by others. We believed and had faith in these ideas—maybe for our whole lives.

We already have enough faith, but where do we direct it? Find out. Notice. And if it's going in a negative direction, redirect it.

Don't look for answers outside of yourself; go within to find your faith. It has been there all along, waiting to be used in a new, positive direction, toward your highest good.

Step 3—Made a decision to turn our will and our lives over to the care of God, as we understood God.

Step 3 asks us to decide. Nothing else. Just decide. The steps that follow are where we will do the work, where we take action, to turn our will and our lives over to the care of a Higher Power.

"Our will" is everything we think and feel.

"Our lives" are everything we say and do.

In other words, our will and our lives are everything about us.

What is this power greater than us? This step says: "as we understood God"—so it is whatever we say She/He/It is. No one can impose a definition on us. We say what this creative intelligence is for us. It just needs to be good—and not us.

Step 3 clearly says that this Higher Power is good—that God cares for us. God wants the best for us. The Universe is looking out for us. Spirit has our backs.

There is no one right way to do Step 3. Do it however it suits you. Personally, I had to be grounded in Step 2. I had to "come to believe" God is good, and that everything that came into my life was designed lovingly for my highest and best good—even if it looked and felt awful and scary and was really not welcome!

> *"There are only two ways to live your life. One is as though nothing is a miracle. The other is as though everything is a miracle."*
> — Albert Einstein

A Course in Miracles states: What could you not accept, if you but knew that everything that happens, all events, past, present, and to come, are gently planned by One Whose only purpose is your good? (*A Course in Miracles: Workbook for Students*, Lesson 135).

The Big Book says, "When we became alcoholics, crushed by a self-imposed crisis we could not postpone or evade, we had to fearlessly face the proposition that either God is everything or else He is nothing. God either is, or He isn't. What was our choice to be?"

Later it says:

> So our troubles, we think, are basically of our own making. They arise out of ourselves, and…we must be rid of this selfishness…. God makes that possible…. We had to have God's help…[so] we decided that hereafter in this drama of life, God was going to be our Director.
>
> When we sincerely took such a position, all sorts of remarkable things followed. We had a new Employer. Being all powerful, He provided what we needed, if

we kept close to Him and performed His work well. Established on such a footing we became less and less interested in ourselves, our little plans and designs. More and more we became interested in seeing what we could contribute to life. As we felt new power flow in, as we enjoyed peace of mind, as we discovered we could face life successfully, as we became conscious of His presence, we began to lose our fear of today, tomorrow or the hereafter. We were reborn.

Take Step 3. Decide. It's just another form of surrender. The decision implies that God is in charge; God's "care" is yours, and it is absolute. We never have to do things or face difficulties on our own. We never need to suffer or be afraid or lonely.... Unless we choose to be!

We have an all-knowing, all-powerful, ever-present source of comfort, guidance, and love, which cares about us unceasingly. Knowing this can be a major turning point in our journey.

The Truth Is: God's love is eminently useful and practical in every situation.

The fact of God as a source for guidance and direction is not theoretical; it is practical and useable in every situation. Maybe we believe it while we are in church, but then we forget it during our weekly routine.

Deciding to turn things over during our daily routine and amid difficulties is the height of practical spirituality.

Decide to let God run the show. Turn it all over to God's care. See how your life works more smoothly and effortlessly than it ever has before. Step 3 is the doorway to a new way of living.

Take the easy way. Take Step 3 by....

Turning It All Over

Part of my life story centers around several health challenges. Working with spiritual principles I learned at Unity Church in Albany, New York, and from other teachers along other spiritual paths, I have not only survived, but have thrived.

In August 1996, I was diagnosed with HIV/AIDS.

In January 2016, I was treated for Stage IV non-Hodgkin's lymphoma.

I have been diagnosed with type-2 diabetes and high blood pressure.

By the Grace of God, I have been in remission from active addiction/alcoholism since January 16, 1995.

Any one of those five diseases are, according to conventional thinking, fatal and insurmountable. Yet today, all are in remission, thanks to God, modern medicine, holistic medicine—and these unfailing, consistent, practical spiritual principles, which work on anyone's health challenges, finances, everything!

The Universe is so benevolent and wise that "curses" become miraculous, beautiful gifts—when we are willing to look past appearances and apply spiritual principles "in all our affairs."

This is what *Prosperity Now!* is all about. These spiritual principles can be applied to any and every situation. In my recovery, I have also been through a divorce; I quit smoking cigarettes; I moved to Paris, France; I owned two houses; I survived bosses who wanted me fired and jobs I hated; I thrived anyway.

I have enjoyed jobs and had bosses I absolutely adored; I was an elected official; I became an ordained minister; I retired young; I have been through many other life events, large and small, all thanks to the spiritual laws we are talking about here, including the surrender and assurance of Step 3.

I have not done Step 3 perfectly by any means. I made a lot of missteps, balked, resisted, backslid, and stubbornly refused to give up old ways. Rest assured, practice makes progress. Willingness and persistence will win the day.

Step 3 shows us that turning every thought, belief, feeling, and deed over to a benevolent, loving Higher Power is the way to freedom and a charmed life. All difficulties can and will be overcome.

You don't need tragic or life-threatening events to drive you to God, but life does have a way of directing us toward our destiny. That destiny can always be one of tremendous good, abundance, peace, and serenity—if we cooperate and turn it all over to God.

The Truth Is:

> "We are certain that God wants us to be happy, joyous, and free."
> — The Big Book

Whenever someone tells me they don't know what God's will is for them, I point to that quote. For me, I don't need any other understanding of God's will. I know my Higher Power wants me to be happy, joyous, and free. And so, I work Step 3 by deciding I will act, think, and feel based on that premise. You don't need to *do* anything just yet. You just need to decide.

ACTION ITEMS
Continue saying, "I am prosperous"

Say it aloud to yourself in a mirror, twenty-five times, three times per day.

Continue reciting your denial and affirmation statements

Keep them in a place where you see them regularly and subconsciously. Patience and persistence pay off. Even if this work feels like it is rote repetition and memorization, it is really working below the surface of your thoughts to break up the old, calcified thinking of the past to ready the soil, planting new, fresh, vibrant ideas that will grow.

This is the faith described in the parable of the mustard seed. From the tiniest seed, with time and persistence, the mustard seed grows into a bush of tremendous size. Your consciousness, your faith, will too.

Statement of Surrender

Continue to say, "I surrender to the innate wisdom of the Universe that resides in me." Feel the excitement and the relief as you rely less on your own limited power and understanding and move into a relationship with a Greater Power and a Higher Understanding that is available to us all.

Begin to Notice

Whenever you say, "I am," what words and thoughts follow? Don't fight these thoughts. Do not get angry or beat yourself up. Just notice what follows whenever you say, "I am."

In which direction does your faith flow? Notice where you put your faith. Is this the direction you want it to go?

Gently notice where your mind, words, and faith go. Is their path working?

Take your Step 3

How? By deciding. By simply making the decision. It really is simple and uncomplicated. However, the decision, once made, needs to be reinforced again and again. It needs to be made again, and again, and again....

The decision is easy. But sticking to it and remembering can take some work. When we backslide and recommit, we change the course of our life.

We are shrinking thoughts of fear and lack and building trust and faith. We become more aware that the Universe wants only our good. God has our good in store for us, and we choose to accept it.

You can take Step 3 with another person, a sponsor, or a trusted friend. Get support for your decision from people who know and who understand. Write it down. Feel the joy and release of knowing you never have to handle any life decision alone ever again. You have the Universe's inherent wisdom within you—ready, willing, and able to guide you to your highest good.

Create a vision statement for yourself

Last week, we defined what mission and vision statements are. Now, create a vision statement for yourself. Remember that a vision statement focuses on tomorrow, on what we want to become.

Your goal should be in line with your mission and vision statements. This is how we integrate all the separate parts of our being. We are learning to grow in integrity and aligning with the Universe, which is always supporting us for our highest and best good.

Reread Week 3 at Least Twice

Tithe—Divine Love, flowing through me, blesses and multiplies all that I have, all that I give and all that I receive. We are blessed to know that Spirit is our Source. God bless! Thank you, God!

Sing

"I Am So Blessed"
by Karen Drucker

I Am so blessed
I Am so blessed
I Am so grateful, for all that I have
I Am so blessed, I Am so blessed
I Am so grateful, I Am so blessed

We are so blessed
We are so blessed
We are so grateful, for all that we have
We are so blessed, We are so blessed
We are so grateful, We are so blessed

God bless! Thank you, God!

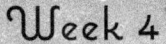

Week 4
Stepping Out of Your Comfort Zone

*Whether you think you can,
or you think you can't, you're right.*
— Henry Ford

Faith Is the Key

A LITTLE MORE ABOUT faith before we move on.

Faith and belief are not synonymous. Faith is like a key that starts a car engine. Faith powers up the Universe's potential. Faith is energy ("Use the Force, Luke!"), and it is activated by belief. Faith will manifest whatever you believe you deserve. Faith will bring you whatever you expect.

Belief is a vibrational level of thought or awareness. Faith unlocks the potential of the Universe and conforms to our belief. Faith is a substance shaped and formed by belief, manifesting whatever it is we believe.

The Truth Is: Belief *activates* faith.

Once the key is turned, faith sets the wheels of the Universe in motion, bringing whatever we believe into existence.

Most people hold unconscious, subconscious beliefs, which end up being fulfilled. *Prosperity Now!* is designed to help us wake up so we can direct this process toward better outcomes. Making the belief/faith connection conscious yields better results—the results we want.

What are your hidden beliefs? What are the "truths" active in your subconscious, giving you the life you have today?

Remember: Our lives proceed from our thoughts. Things don't so much happen *to* us as *through* us. Beyond that, life happens *from* us and, most importantly, *all things* happen *for* us!

Making Unconscious Beliefs Conscious

We want to make our unconscious beliefs conscious, examine them, change them, or replace them with healthier, more abundant ideas and beliefs. Many beliefs we hold were not originally ours; they are often untrue childhood messages and need to be replaced. Old beliefs, active in our minds and hearts, bring us all manner of "stuff," much not good or chosen consciously.

Remember: You have all the faith you need. Are you in touch with it? Where are you directing it? For example, believing we are unlucky activates our faith from that perspective. Then we will see examples everywhere "proving" and reinforcing our beliefs unconsciously. And our world and lives will reflect it.

Turn the key of faith consciously, with thoughtful, clear objectives!

The Truth Is: The Universe is benevolent. It is always on our side.

Goodness of the Universe vs. Tragedies of the World

There is good in every situation. This powerful statement may seem wildly off the mark given the tragedies and suffering in the world, yet we can come to believe that Universal Goodness is present in every situation, even when things seem bad. Especially then, really.

Temporal and spiritual mysteries have been pondered for centuries. Why is there suffering? Why is there death? Why do bad things happen to good people?

These deep, philosophical, and spiritual dilemmas are not answered by trite phrases and pop-spiritual axioms.

"Well, if you just look at the bright side...."

"You just have to pray harder...."

"You must be doing something wrong. Maybe you're not saying your affirmations right or with enough faith, etc."

Spiritual Malpractice!

I say it is "spiritual malpractice" to say these things to someone who is confused, hurting, in pain, suffering, or grieving. There are deeper and more complex truths than we can know. Mystery remains mystery.

The spiritual principles we are learning may not put to rest the great puzzles of existence. Human experience is one of tremendous extremes. Joy is joy. Grief is grief. Sadness is sadness. Love is love. Pain is pain.

Living in harmony with God's laws, we can help people, lessening misery and increasing joy. We can be less like someone "poor in Spirit," and be more of a spiritual seeker—increasing abundance, happiness, and freedom for ourselves and everyone else.

I can testify that times I have suffered have yielded much more good than pain. Tragedies I experienced—once I learned to "see them right"—became sources for tremendous insight and spiritual gifts.

I believe—I know—that in any tragedy, the good that ensues equals the "bad," plus more good! The results are always a net increase of God/Good in the world.

One story and two examples from my life may help illustrate my point.

Willie

In September 1991, my twenty-five-year-old partner, Willie, died of AIDS-related complications. At that time, I was an active addict, lost emotionally, financially, mentally, and most of all, spiritually.

His death ended a summer when my car was repossessed, I lost my home and, to put salt in the wounds, I had to have two teeth pulled. To describe the wretchedness and sadness I felt would be difficult. Alone, homeless, sleeping on a friend's sofa, flat broke, and in total despair, I had no support, no spiritual understanding, no prospects, and no hope.

But just four years later, I was clean and sober; I had gainful employment at the start of a marvelous career; I had a wealth of friends; I had hope!

What changed? I had begun, in my misery and poverty, to walk a spiritual path. I started down this road not because I was a saint, but because I had the Gift of Desperation (G.O.D.) that we spoke about in Week 1.

Willie's death was a tragedy, but was it in vain? No! His death touched many people. It personally propelled me into a new life with purpose and direction. Would I have sought God without such pain? Not likely.

Sa'mone

In 2013, my then-husband, Mark, and I had a beautiful Yorkshire terrier, Sa'mone. She was a bright light for many people. Sa'mone marched in parades with me when I was a local politician. Even today, people still talk about her as a memorable part of our community.

When she was ten years old, someone brought a dog into our house, and it attacked and killed Sa'mone. To say our grief was intense is an understatement. That small, five-pound dog left an immense hole in our lives, in our house, and in our hearts.

After one week, I couldn't stand it. I went online to Petfinders.com to look at Yorkshire terriers. I saw a needy-looking dog named Morton Morkie. I showed my husband. He said, "Well, call them." So, I did.

Morton's foster mom, in her Georgia accent, said, "All he wants to do is be held." Oh, great! I filled out the paperwork.

The adoption process was almost complete when the Georgia Mom said, "Well, we got'a little girl here, too. She's stinkin' cute."

I said, "She's what?"

"She's stinkin' cute!"

"Send me a picture."

She said, "If I send you a picture, you're gonna want her."

A week later, a Delta cargo plane from Atlanta, Georgia, brought two dogs who quickly went from Morton and Tina to Manny and Erica.

Sa'mone died horribly, generating tremendous sadness and grief in our world and for the many people who knew her. A reporter even wrote a newspaper column about her because she touched many people's lives.

Was Sa'mone's death in vain? No! Manny and Erica in foster care needed homes. Manny especially needed rehabilitation. Sa'mone's death opened space for them. And, looking back, Sa'mone came into our lives just when we needed her, and she left just when she was supposed to.

In life and in their tragic deaths, both Willie and Sa'mone created more good and more joy than sadness and sorrow. Pain, sorrow, and sadness are difficult and overwhelming, but the Way of the Universe is such that good always arises from tragedy, good that is always greater than the "bad."

In time, the "bad" is just a memory, but the Good still flows as strong as ever!

When musician Lou Reed died, his wife, poet Laurie Anderson said, "The purpose of death is to release love."

Think about that. All our love is lying there, unexpressed, in potential. If we "see it right," we experience love pouring out in our grief—love that was there all along, waiting to be expressed.

But what about those who suffer tragedy? What about people who lose their lives or go through traumatic experiences?

Once, a mystic told me, "Just because someone we pray for dies, don't ever think they didn't get the miracle they needed."

There is a much larger picture than we can see with our human eyes. Trust that God is all-good, that we are cared for and protected. When the world throws us a giant mess, a tragedy, or an unexpected sorrow, at some point, we can move through the feelings toward a place of peace, acceptance, and faith that goodness and love are there for us and for everyone affected.

The Greatest Illusion

Once there was a Zen Master whose greatest lesson to her students was: Life is an illusion. Suffering is an illusion. Existence is an illusion. Permanence is an illusion. Everything is an illusion.

The master was a great teacher who attracted many disciples.

One day, the master's child died suddenly. The students looked but could not find her. Finally, in a quiet, hidden place in the monastery's garden, they found their master weeping uncontrollably.

Although most of the students were overcome with compassion, one couldn't help himself, "You teach everything is an illusion. Isn't your child's death also an illusion?"

"Yes," replied the master. "It is an illusion. But it is by far the greatest illusion of them all."

"Know the Truth, but respect the illusion," is a wonderful saying that encapsulates a fundamental paradox: We will see and experience things in life that conflict with spiritual reality. This phrase can help us to keep a deeper perspective, put things in their proper perspective. We can experience the deep lows and the giddy highs of this world, feeling our deep feelings fully. And, all the while understand there is a greater purpose, a larger picture, and a "Kingdom of Heaven" that is the ultimate reality.

By knowing and respecting that illusion is in opposition to spiritual reality, we can manifest our good and handle difficult situations. Remember Mary Morrissey's *Prosperity Plus* phrase, "I am so happy and grateful now that...."? How would you fill in the blank?

Another example from my life can illustrate how this works to turn away from old beliefs (that things won't work out) to create in our minds a conscious assurance that things will manifest in miraculous ways for my highest and best good.

How I Manifested My Perfect, Permanent Place in Paris

At sixty years old, I had never lived outside of New York State. Moving from my small hometown to the state capital, Albany, in 1990 was a big deal for me, although it was only fifty miles away. So moving to Paris, France, was well outside of my comfort zone

All my life, I had doubts and fears (beliefs) that things would not work out. This was how I saw the world. My strong faith was against anything good, amazing, or wonderful being possible—and it was all unconscious. I never thought I could try something as daunting as moving out of the country. But by 2017, I had done a lot of work in recovery and affirmative prayer. "New Thought" principles of abundance and the goodness of God slowly gave me a newfound confidence.

I believed things would work out well for me.

The Truth Is: "Things always work out well for me because God is with me in every situation."

This is one of my go-to affirmations. I know my Higher Power always has my best interests at heart and will move mountains to help me fulfill my dreams.

Moving to Paris took two years of planning: settling things in New York, renting out my house, dealing with health and health insurance, ensuring I could get a full supply of medications, traveling with two dogs, the French visa process, finding a place to live in Paris, etc. Each step was an opportunity to shed old beliefs and point my faith in a new direction.

Metaphysically and spiritually, for the Universe to fulfill my ideas, I need to have clear and specific goals. What kind of apartment did I want?

I used Morrissey's phrase to create a clear idea, which I could believe: "I am so happy and grateful now that I have my perfect, permanent place in Paris, in an old, cut-stone building, with plenty of space, light, and air."

My budget was modest. I kept repeating (and believing with faith) my affirmation, throwing in some French phrases: "I am so happy and grateful now that I have my perfect, permanent place in Paris *dans un immeuble, pierre de taillée, avec beaucoup d'espace, lumière et d'air.*"

I looked at some apartments. None were suitable. Worse, my realtor never said I would need a bank account *and* up to a year's rent in advance to secure a place.

Time grew short, but Higher Power was on the case. And my faith was activated in the right direction. A cousin called one day. His friends had an apartment available immediately. I called them several times, but they were on vacation and difficult to reach. Finally, we connected. They said their tenant would show me the place...but she was on vacation and difficult to reach.

I went to explore the neighborhood in a very elegant section of Paris, the sixteenth arrondissement, an area I had considered out of my league.

I went inside the building's foyer. When I came out, *voila!* I had a phone message from the current tenant. She had called me just when I was standing at her door.

I saw the place. It was almost exactly what I prayed for—bigger than I envisioned, and more money than I budgeted for, but within my means.

It was unfurnished, which was not my prayer, an important wrinkle. I had envisioned a furnished apartment, so, if things didn't work out, I could just pack up and leave. An unfurnished apartment meant buying furniture—an investment in the future—and permanence.

I believe I was given an unfurnished place so I would know God planned for me to *really* be in Paris.

After I moved in, I bought my first plant, another conscious action saying I had a real long-term home. Gulp.

And two things topped off the miracle:

1. Bank accounts are difficult to open for foreigners. When I went to the landlord's bank to put down my deposit on the apartment, a banker asked me if I wanted to open an account. Did I ever! My apartment got me a French bank account!
2. This happened in August, when *nothing* happens in France. Everyone goes on vacation for four to five weeks; very little business gets done.

Friends who have lived in France for decades were amazed I was so "lucky" getting such a lovely, large, elegant space in Paris—and in August. However, I am certain luck played no part in it. It was all God and faith.

Pronoia

I first heard this term from Rob Brezsny in *Real Astrology*, a weekly astrology column unlike any you've read before.

We all know what paranoid people believe: "They're out to get me." Paranoid people see trouble and conspiracy everywhere. They believe they're in danger. The world, the government, the mob, or aliens are out to get them. That is no way to live and be happy.

Me? I am a "pronoic." I encourage you to be one too. What is pronoia? Pronoics believe the world is out to *help* them. God is on their side. The Universe and everyone is conspiring to bring them their good.

Every event, no matter how it first appears, comes to me, and through me, for my highest and best good. A pronoic attitude is powerful, happy, healing, healthy, and whole. Imagine it. No longer are we victims of the world, of people, places, things, and circumstances. Now we are certain that all of life is on our side. We are in the flow of a mighty stream of substance, to paraphrase Eric Butterworth.

Everyone and everything is in a vast, wonderful conspiracy to help me wake up. They all care about me, want the best for me, and are leading me to my highest and best good. Our most difficult relationships are teachers, mirroring back to us negative energies that we need to be rid of. Our most difficult circumstances are pulling (or pushing) us to get off the spot where we are and move us in a new direction, to a new place, think a new thought, take positive action we might never have taken if circumstances were not so dire.

Alcoholics and other twelve-steppers will assert that their worst day turned out to be their best day when seen in retrospect. It was G.O.D. (Gift of Desperation) that "forced" them to change, to wake up, to move to consider a new possibility—one that seemed impossible, foolish, or too much to ask.

Practicing pronoia, we are directing our faith rightly, leading to our highest good. Instead of asking: Why is this person messing with me? Why does this always happen to me? How come I must endure this awful situation or this "bad break," ask: How is this situation or person here to help me?

The beautiful part is: You don't need an answer. All you need to do is become aware of the question, and then just sit with it. Let the innate wisdom of the Universe residing in you show you the answer. With a little time and open-mindedness, it will come.

The Truth Is: This situation (or person or circumstance) is not here to hurt me. It is here to teach me and help me grow!

Another way of asking the question comes from songwriter, Mark Shepard, who posed the question this way: How does this situation turn out better than I expected?

Inherent in the question is the positive, pronoic assumption that this situation *will* turn out better than I expect. Guaranteed. Again, it is important to sit with the question. It is not necessary to contrive an answer. Ego wants an answer, and ego wants *its* answer.

We allow the Universe to provide the answer, so have patience. Wait in delicious anticipation, because we are pronoic, and we know things always work out well for us.

Motto

By now, you are well on your way to completing your mission and vision statements. This is a process worth spending some time on. These guiding stars will help you steer in the direction of your dreams.

Now we will want to add a motto—something short, sharp, pithy, and enlivened with zest and zeal. We want a motto that captures who we are, and who we are striving to become!

I remember my motto and check in with it whenever I feel I am off base. If you recall, my motto is: *Vivez joyeaux!* (Live joyously, or Live with joy!)

When I am feeling impatient, uncharitable, put-upon, like a victim, engaged in a task that feels like a chore or otherwise not my best self, at some point—hopefully sooner rather than later—my motto comes to mind, and I recalibrate my attitude.

Am I living joyously? Am I *being* joyous? Am I reflecting my highest self?

Your motto should be a snappy bumper sticker for your life. It is an easy, shorthand way to describe—to your conscious mind, your subconscious mind, to the world at large, and to the Universe—exactly who and what you are and what you desire to become.

Step 4—Made a searching and fearless moral inventory of ourselves.

(Clearing out clutter)

Denials clear out our mind's cluttered room, our weed-filled garden. Step 4 continues and deepens that process.

To expand your consciousness and develop new ways of thinking, you must trade old, useless, tired, ineffective ideas for fresh, new, vital ones. The Bible has many parables and metaphors for this. One I like is:

> "And no one puts new wine into old wineskins. For the wine would burst the wineskins, and the wine and the skins would both be lost. New wine calls for new wineskins."
>
> — Mark 2:22

Travelers in those days knew that a leather bag (metaphysically, our consciousness) to hold wine (ideas) couldn't be reused. The leather would have shrunk. Refilling the bag would stretch the wineskin until it burst.

The plain meaning holds a deeper truth: You cannot put new ideas (wine) into an old consciousness (wineskin)! New ideas need a changed mind.

The old consciousness just can't hold a new idea—it can't conceive of the possibilities. Explain snow to someone in the tropics.

The word "Repent" means "rethink." Simple. Profound. Rethink. Think again. Change your mind. Think of something newer and truer.

In Step 4, we take stock, inventorying our minds and lives, our thinking and behavior, carefully and thoroughly. What are your ideas and beliefs? What is old, stale, and useless? What is useable, vibrant, fresh, and worth keeping? Anything not worth keeping throw it out, making room for new, better ideas!

Clear out the weeds and rocks in your garden so you can plant healthy and life-giving thoughts that will grow to be tremendous assets in the days ahead.

This step calls for writing. Use your Prosperity Journal to write your inventory. The act of writing takes what's inside us—where it is formless and indeterminate—and makes it concrete, pinning it down to be examined clearly.

Remember: Our thoughts create our actions; actions become habits, making up the pattern of our lives.

An inventory is not an emotional exercise, but a clear-eyed look at ourselves, "a fact-finding and a fact-facing process," as *The Big Book* calls it.

Think of a storekeeper going through the shelves. What is good and can be displayed? What is broken or old, needing to be discarded?

Pay special attention to fears and resentments. Where have we been selfish? Where have we been afraid? Where, when, and with whom have we been less than our best selves—and why?

When someone did us wrong, more importantly, what was our part in the matter?

Another area to list is character defects that cause us trouble. Are we selfish? Are we angry? Impatient? Judgmental? Greedy? Stubborn? List all these negative traits, but also list our character assets.

Are we generous? Are we brave? Are we thoughtful? Kind and compassionate? Quick to forgive? Serene? Helpful to others? Our list of character assets will be longer than the list of negative character traits. Guaranteed! If it is not longer, keep looking. You missed some very good qualities about yourself. Ask other people what they see in you that is wonderful. Believe them.

The inventory is important because it brings up—to be healed—all the hidden, secret, and heavy things from our past that are inside our subconscious mind, negatively affecting our lives and choices today. The inventory shows us where we need work, where we fall short. It also shows us where our strengths lie. This is very important to know!

We cannot put new ideas into an old consciousness. We must "change our minds" (repent) to take new ideas into our hearts where they can direct our lives and our choices.

Be Gentle with Yourself

It is very important to be gentle with ourselves in this process. We must not beat ourselves up over our past thoughts, words, or deeds. Inventories give us a clearer look at who we have been so we can change, grow, and be better. It is a clear-eyed stock-taking. Shame, remorse, and guilt have no place here. We are moving toward new horizons, gaining new ways, leaving the old behind. The past has no power over us!

We surrendered; we are coming to believe; we made a decision; and now we are cleaning house. The past will not drag us down anymore. We are lifting ourselves up to be the free, light, abundant, and creative spirits we are meant to be.

Zones—Comfort, Learning, and Panic

As a student at the Harvard's Kennedy School of Government, Senior Executives program, I was privileged to meet some of the world's best and brightest. We spent one full day on Thompson's Island in the middle of Boston Harbor for an Outward Bound-type experience.

One activity we did was to climb a swinging ladder—long, unstable beams suspended high above a gymnasium floor by heavy steel cables. In teams of four—strapped in safety harnesses, with another team on the ground holding rappelling ropes—we climbed the swaying structure.

I am not very athletic, but for some reason, my team had me go first. I clambered onto the first rung; then we helped each other climb up. The boards we stood on were narrow and very wobbly—and each level was higher up than the last, so the climb got more difficult.

The final level was so high that there was no way to reach the top without letting go of everything below—everything that kept me "safe." I had one shot! I had to stand straight up to grab the highest rung on the ladder. If I missed, I would be swinging in the air by the rappelling ropes. (Hopefully, the team on the ground was paying attention!)

After consulting with my group, I counted—one-two-three—and lunged up with a push from my team to grab the top rung. Success! What a thrilling feeling! It was exhilaration and achievement like I'd never known before.

Later, our instructor taught us something I'll never forget, which you can use in this course. It will help you gauge where you are in the process at any given time, so you can adjust accordingly. There are three zones we can be in:

1. The Comfort Zone, where we usually live, but we don't learn much there. We don't make progress or grow or change.
2. The Learning Zone is outside of our Comfort Zone. There, we are out on a limb (so to speak). We are in a new arena where we don't know very much.
3. The Panic Zone, where we will not learn anything either! The Panic Zone is so far away from our Comfort Zone we can actually experience physical symptoms: sweat, cold feet, shortness of breath, dizziness, stress, and even terror. When we find ourselves in the Panic Zone, we need to recognize it and immediately pull back.

We do not learn anything in either the comfort or the panic zones. Also, it is better to leave the comfort zone willingly and on purpose to venture into the learning zone, where we can remain safely for a while, exploring, stretching, and testing our minds and hearts, our ideas and beliefs. Then, return to the comfort zone for rest and rejuvenation.

The miracle is that doing this consciously expands our comfort zone. A larger comfort zone gives us more room, more space, more light, and more freedom—in our minds and in our lives.

Things that in the past might have made us panic move into our learning zone and become interesting places to explore. Things that were once curious and unfamiliar are now in our comfort zone—aka, been there; done that.

We all know people—maybe ourselves—whose lives are very narrow. They may never travel far from home, never vary from their routine, maybe for years, even decades.

The Truth Is: If we don't choose to leave our comfort zone, life will choose for us. Fate will intervene. Events will come to shake us up, get us moving. Sadly, it is often something tragic or difficult or upsetting, the "Crash and Burn" experience we spoke about. Inevitably, life will grab us to shake us awake.

We cannot safely hide forever in our comfort zone. It is better to choose to leave it willingly, knowing safety is assured by our Higher Power.

Rob Brezsny, in his *Astrology Newsletter*, writes about this phenomenon:

> Prediction: As an aspiring lover of pronoia, you will have a growing knack for gravitating toward wilder, wetter, more interesting problems. More and more, you will be drawn to the kind of gain that doesn't require pain. You'll be so alive and awake that you'll cheerfully push yourself out of your comfort zone in the direction of your personal frontier well before you're forced to do so by divine kicks in the ass.

That is what you do when you choose to tithe, despite some fear. Or when you move to another state or country, go back to school, or start a new career mid-life. Or when you go on a date, attend a new social group, start a new hobby, or speak up for yourself or another, even if your voice shakes.

Although I love playing guitar and singing, at one time the idea of getting up in front of people was terrifying. I *knew* I would have a panic attack if I made even one mistake. I would (I thought) literally die of embarrassment.

With encouraging friends, I played guitar and sang a song with someone at church. Then I did a solo song. My voice shook and cracked. I thought I wouldn't get through it. But I did, and the fear lessened. I now enjoy playing and singing. I still have some anxiety, but I usually muster up the courage and feel the exhilaration and joy afterward.

Breathe. Watch fear turn to excitement and joyous anticipation. Your courage by taking action, expanding your consciousness, puts new wine in new wineskins.

ACTION ITEMS
Explore Your Comfort and Learning Zones

See what each feels like. See what it feels like to move between the two. If you go into the panic zone, ease up until you feel safe again.

This exercise can be practiced in many areas: with family and friends, in social situations, at work, in stores and restaurants, etc. Notice when you have stayed too long in the comfort zone and intentionally move yourself out into the learning zone before the Universe does it for you.

Write in your prosperity journal what these zones are like for you. Write about your adventures in the Learning Zone and any time you might have stumbled into the Panic Zone. Journaling these experiences will give you much information to look back on, to see how far you have come.

Write out your Step 4 inventory

Resentments, fears, defects, and assets. Write as much as you can, being fearless and thorough. This is a key step! Remove the old so the new can take root.

Remember: Be easy on yourself and keep sight of the goal—a new and better you and a new and better life, full of all the Good the Universe has to offer! Ask for help from someone who has done this before. They have valuable experience to share and can help you avoid mistakes they might have made.

Create a Motto for yourself

In Week 2, we discussed mission and vision statements. Now create a motto, a bumper sticker, that encapsulates your purpose or guiding principle. Take your time with this. Allow yourself to be led by Spirit to the perfect zinger for you, a motto that oozes life, love, joy, and purpose!

Review your twelve-week goal; see if you are moving in that direction

It is important to check in on your goal throughout the course. You want to keep journaling about the goal, adding details, embellishing, thinking about what the next step on the journey is.

Goals often need to be modified, tweaked, or overhauled altogether in the light of new information about ourselves or about circumstances and priorities. Don't be afraid to be flexible while working in partnership with the Universe, which will not let us fail, but will gently guide us in the direction of our dreams and our highest and best good.

Reread Week 4 at Least Twice

> ***Tithe****—Divine Love, flowing through me, blesses and multiplies all that I have, all that I give, and all that I receive. We are blessed to know Spirit is our Source. God bless! Thank you, God!*

Sing

> "I Am So Blessed"
> by Karen Drucker
>
> I Am so blessed
> I Am so blessed
> I Am so grateful, for all that I have
> I Am so blessed, I Am so blessed
> I Am so grateful, I Am so blessed

We are so blessed
We are so blessed
We are so grateful, for all that we have
We are so blessed, We are so blessed
We are so grateful, We are so blessed

God bless! Thank you, God!

Week 5

Begin It Now
(and Don't Ask How)

Our job is not to set things right, but to see things right.
— Eric Butterworth

Law of Circulation

YOU PROBABLY LEARNED about the water cycle in school. It is helpful to think of our lives and our prosperity as using a similar model.

Water evaporates into the atmosphere where it concentrates as clouds. Then it falls back down as rain or snow, feeding the ground, nourishing plants, animals, people, and all life.

A river flows to the sea where the water evaporates. It rains at the headwaters of the river; the process starts all over again. There is an abundance of water on the planet; fresh water is consistently and reliably replenished.

But suppose the water cycle breaks down. Suppose a river gets silted up, so clogged with mud and debris it slows until it is finally choked off altogether. Or suppose a region's weather patterns change so no rain falls there anymore. It would eventually become a desert, and life would be challenging.

The outflow of water is a crucial part of the water cycle. Water must leave the ocean and evaporate up. Water must leave the river to replenish the ocean. For the cycle to work, water must...well...it has to *cycle*, in *and* out.

If the supply is cut off, the result is a desert, a drought, a muddy, lifeless river.

If there is no consistent, reliable outflow, the result is similar. A buildup of water without release results in a stagnant and lifeless situation. A dead sea.

This same phenomenon holds true for everything in life and consciousness.

The supply of all good—life, health, serenity, joy, love, fellowship, creative energies, meaningful work, family, friends, food, drink, money, spiritual growth, pleasure, generosity, intellectual stimulation—all of life's vitality comes to us from anywhere and everywhere....

For the supply to flow, we must keep the channel open. We have a decided part. We are the ones responsible for clearing a path—in consciousness—that will widen and deepen, resulting in an ever-increasing flow of good.

Remember: Good can come to us through many channels, but there is only One Source, God—the Universe—supplies all of our good. Our lives are enriched.

Knowing this makes things simple and direct. We don't need to focus on all the details—or what Taoists call, "The Ten-Thousand Things." All we must do is focus on the One Source, which will meet all our needs, wants, and desires.

To ensure the supply is not interrupted, we must keep the channel open in our mind. Increase cannot come to a stream that is dammed up. More good cannot come to a mind that is closed. The Law of Circulation requires a free and uninhibited exchange.

An electrical plug has prongs allowing the current to flow in and out. A complete circuit is necessary. Interrupt the circuit and the electricity stops. It cannot flow because the circulation is impeded.

The famous dancer and choreographer, Martha Graham, wrote a letter to her friend, fellow dancer and choreographer Agnes de Mille. At the time, de Mille was very discouraged. Graham expressed something profound for every artist, for every creative spirit. She wrote:

> There is a vitality, a life force, a quickening that is translated through you into action, and because there is only one of you in all time, this expression is unique. And if you block it, it will never exist through any other

medium, and it will be lost. The world will not have it.

It is not your business to determine how good it is, nor how valuable it is, nor how it compares with other expressions. It is your business to keep it yours clearly and directly, to keep the channel open. You do not even have to believe in yourself or your work. You have to keep open and aware directly to the urges that motivate you. Keep the channel open.

With all things spiritual or financial, with our health, to become and remain serene, to live life creatively—in everything—we must stay attached to Source. We must connect to the energy, the Spirit, the good for it to flow through us. We must broaden, widen, and deepen the channel to keep it open!

This Law of Circulation is expressed in yet another way, as....

The Law of Giving and Receiving

> *"In all things, remember.... 'It is more blessed to give than to receive.'"*
> — Acts 20:35

At some point, a child's training can dampen their natural spirit of generosity. You may have seen an older child (and many adults) who would rather get a gift than give away one of their toys. Often in spiritual matters, what seems to be true is 180 degrees away from what is really true in Spirit.

A Course in Miracles puts it this way:

> **Lesson 108: To give and to receive are one in truth.**
>
> Vision depends upon today's idea. The light is in it, for it reconciles all seeming opposites.... And now you are at peace forever, for the dream is over then.
>
> True light that makes true vision possible is not the light the body's eyes behold. It is a state of mind that has become so unified that darkness cannot be perceived at all.... This is the light that shows no opposites, and vision, being healed, has power to heal.

Knowing this, your peace of mind is unshakable! You will realize and demonstrate that there is no opposition in Spirit. You cannot lose anything of value because you *are* the giver *and* the receiver.

We are a part of this *Uni-verse*. As such, in truth we are all one. Giving in Spirit, we give to ourselves. Receiving, we receive that which we already possess—difficult concepts for the human mind to grasp, difficult for the body's eyes to see. But our souls recognize the light, the energy in this idea.

Any artist knows this truth when they give their gift to the public. After a performance or an exhibition, they may be exhausted physically. But emotionally, creatively, and spiritually, they will say they feel more energy, more wellbeing, more enthusiasm, not less.

Anyone in twelve-step recovery knows this concept well: We can only keep what we have by giving it away. In the physical world, giving means losing. I have less; you have more. But in Spirit, what we give away strengthens both giver and receiver.

Because no matter what, what we give is, at its core, an idea. Ideas always increase and are strengthened when shared.

Once given *and* received, two people have the idea; two people *believe* the idea. They begin to *live* the idea and it grows, becoming more powerful as more people believe it and use it in their lives.

Money seems to be bits of paper and metal, or electronic numbers on a screen, but in truth, money is an idea. Money is a concept so powerful we all believe it. We use it. Most of us don't question its reality or its origin. Money is such a common concept that we mostly accept it without question.

Seen in the light of truth, we can now easily understand that the Law of Circulation, of giving and receiving, is powerful. Using it is the way to prosperity.

The *Tao Te Ching* says:

> *The sage does not hoard.*
> *The more he does for others,*
> *The more he has.*
> *The more he thereby gives to others,*
> *The ever more he gets.*
> — Poem 81

Jesus said:

> *Peace I leave you; my peace I give you.*
> *Not as the world gives.*
> *Let not your hearts be troubled,*
> *neither let them be afraid.*
> — John 14:27

The Peace of God is something we can have. When we share peace, it is strengthened in both giver and receiver.

The appearance is: If I give (as the world sees giving), I have lost something.

The reality is: When I give with awareness of the spiritual laws, then all exchanges become an exchange of ideas, transferring spiritual energy. Living this way, I know I always will receive what I give and more.

Finally, the Bible says, "You will reap what you sow."

It doesn't say you will reap *where* you sow. You may help someone out by giving them $10. That doesn't mean you'll get $10 or find $10, or even that the person you gave the $10 to will pay you back!

What spiritually mindful giving means is you have shared an idea of abundance, generosity, and love. Now, you both are tuned into these spiritual concepts. With growing faith, you both will see the world with a more generous spirit. You will feel better about yourself; self-esteem will grow. You will be happier, healthier, more expansive, and ready to grow spiritually.

"God loves a cheerful giver" can be turned around to say: "A cheerful giver loves (is more in tune with) God."

"How" Will This Work?

In Week 1, you were asked to pick a goal to achieve before the end of the program. Hopefully, you have your goal clearly in mind and have it written down where you'll see it often so it permeates your subconscious.

Hopefully, the idea is believable to you but outside of your comfort zone, firmly in the middle of your learning zone (and definitely not in the panic zone).

One natural doubt is: How will this manifest? How could this happen? Inherent in that question are subtle blocks, doubts, and "logical" beliefs, which can cause our faith to go in the wrong direction.

The best answer is: Don't ask how!

"How" a goal will be achieved is not for you to consider. Faith says leave "how" in the hands of the Creative Intelligence of the Universe. Your job is to name and envision the goal clearly, with faith. Your job is to do whatever is next on the list to move toward your goal: Make that phone call, write out your plan, research the topic, find the expert, pray, save money, etc.

Philosopher Johann von Goethe is rumored to have written, "Whatever you can do or dream you can do, begin it now. Boldness has genius, power, and magic in it. Begin it now!"

We may be inclined to worry, hesitate, question, or balk. We may want to know how things will end. That kind of thinking can paralyze us before we start. Those magical words attributed to Goethe urge us to commit—with faith, to trust the benevolent Universe to move with and for us in the direction of our dreams. We only need take the first step.

Why wait for the Universe to pull you out of your comfort zone? Choose to change! You have the power to choose the path.

The entire quote is originally credited to Scotsman William Hutchison Murray, an early mountaineer and author of many inspirational books. It deserves to be repeated in full:

> Until one is committed, there is hesitancy, the chance to draw back, always ineffectiveness. Concerning all acts of initiative and creation, there is one elementary truth the ignorance of which kills countless ideas and splendid plans: that the moment one definitely commits oneself, then providence moves too. All sorts of things occur to help one that would never otherwise have occurred. A whole stream of events issues from the decision, raising in one's favor all manner of unforeseen incidents, meetings, and material assistance which no man could have dreamed would have come his way. Whatever you can do or dream, you can, begin it. Boldness has genius, power, and magic in it. Begin it now.

A different way to express this comes from English essayist Joseph Addison, "He who hesitates is lost."

Trust the innate wisdom that resides in you. Let go and let God!

A pithy shorthand for the idea is: *"Begin it now, and don't ask how."*

How something will manifest is not your concern. Focus on "What?" What can I do now? What's next on my list? What does my gut tell me to do? What can I accomplish today, right now?

The Serenity Prayer can be recited with a twist to release any worry about "how":

> God, grant me the serenity to accept the things I cannot change *here, right now*.
>
> The courage to change the things I can *here, right now*.
>
> And the wisdom to know the difference.

Trust Your Gut—Trust Your Intuition

In my career in legislative affairs, I worked on passing laws and budgets in the New York State Legislature in Albany, New York. I spent considerable time out of my office, walking around the government complex of the state capitol.

Off doing errands, I would listen to my intuition. Without knowing why, a nudge would surface: Get off on the fourth floor. Go see so-and-so. Go right, not left.

Almost without fail, I'd run into someone I needed to see, or catch the person I needed to call. I would meet a friend who gave me necessary information. I had unexpected encounters that solved problems.

None of these things were on my list of errands, but they were vital nonetheless. By paying close attention to the innate wisdom of the Universe within, I had more success at my job than I otherwise might have.

Close Encounters of a Spiritual Kind

One day, I felt an urge to get up from my desk and go across the street to the capitol building, which I did. In the lobby, I saw my friend Heidi, who seemed agitated. I asked her what was wrong.

She raved, "I just met the Dalai Lama! He was just here! He went upstairs to the senate chamber. Wait. He'll come back this way."

I wasn't sure I believed her, but I waited. Sure enough, twenty minutes later, there was His Holiness, the Dalai Lama, and his entourage. He stopped and greeted the dozen or so people in the lobby. He shook my hand! He smiled his beatific smile, and said, "Thank you," to which I could only reply, "Thank you!"

He was thanking me? For what?

Then he left. I went off into a quiet room and tears welled up. To be in his presence was overwhelming and beautiful. I still get emotional when recounting the event.

I cannot stress enough how important it is to fine-tune our ability to listen to the innate wisdom—our intuition—within. It is a vital faculty in your journey to grow your prosperity consciousness.

A few years later, the same thing happened. I heard, "Get up." I listened.

I left my building and headed across to the capitol. It was a quiet August afternoon with few people or cars on the street. I saw a Mercedes limousine do a U-turn and park at the capitol's entrance. A scruffy young man got out and opened the back door. Out stepped Yoko Ono. I was right there, so I went over and said, "Hello, Ms. Ono. Welcome to Albany. It's an honor to see you. I'm a great admirer of you and John."

She didn't say anything but extended her hand, which I took. I was so mesmerized; I didn't recognize that the "scruffy man" was Sean Ono Lennon!

Listen to that intuition. Cultivate an ability to act when it speaks, which it does as *A Course in Miracles* says, "All throughout the day."

Don't Set Things Right, See Things Right

"Happiness is an inside job." Happiness from outside isn't real and doesn't last. The initial happiness of a new car or a new job fades. When things seem wrong, people naturally try and fix their outer circumstances first.

But *setting* things right is not the solution. Learn to *see* things right!

Trying to set things right, we seek to control the world around us. If only our kids would behave, if our partner would do this (or not do that), if our job was different, if our nose was different, if we had more money, etc., our life would be different.

Rearranging the deck chairs on the *Titanic* won't fix what is really an inside problem.

> *"Do not judge by appearances,*
> *but judge with right judgment."*
> — John 7:24.

Using higher-level thinking, look past appearances to truth. Your denials and affirmations will help you do this: denning appearances of lack, illness, or failure will free your mind. Affirmations affirm what is real despite appearances.

A short story from China helps illustrate how to look past appearances:

> A farmer has a horse, a very valuable thing. One day, the horse runs away. The neighbors say, "How terrible to lose your precious horse. Now how will you pull your plow?"
>
> The farmer replies, "Terrible? Who knows?"
>
> Soon after, the horse returns and brings five wild horses with it. Now the farmer has six horses in the corral. The neighbors all say, "What wonderful luck! Now you are richer than before!"
>
> The farmer replies, "Wonderful? Who knows?"
>
> The next week, the farmer's son is taming one of the wild horses. The horse throws him off and he breaks his leg. The neighbors say, "How awful. Your son is injured. Now who will help you around the farm?"
>
> The farmer replies, "Awful? Who knows?"
>
> A week later, the king's soldiers arrive and conscript all the young men to go fight a battle. However, they do not take the farmer's son because he cannot walk.

This is how to look past appearances—by not judging anything as "good" or "bad." Instead, accept. Seen correctly, all things are neutral and we give them meaning. Turn away from appearances to see the spiritual reality.

Remember! The Innate Wisdom of the Universe is good and on our side. We are pronoic. Everything conspires to help us. Deny appearances; focus past appearances to the reality.

The Truth Is: When things "go wrong," we tend only to see what is breaking down and going away. We naturally want to save what seems to be getting lost.

In truth, if you look past immediate events, you will see that something new is coming through for you. Something better. Your good is always expressing itself, in every circumstance.

You can see everything as a blessing—if you see it right!

The *Tao Te Ching*, Poem 20 starts:

> *Renounce knowledge and end your problems.*
> *What is the difference between yes and no?*
> *What is the difference between good and evil?*
> *Must you fear what others fear?*
> *Nonsense. Look how far you have missed the mark!*

There is no difference between opposites, except what we make of them. One can have great success and fail miserably. Another can fail and yet be a great success.

Poem 13 says:

> *Success is as dangerous as failure.*
> *Hope is as hollow as fear.*
> *What does it mean that success is as*
> *dangerous as failure?*
> *Whether you go up the ladder or down it,*
> *your position is shaky.*
> *When you stand with your two feet on the ground,*
> *you will always keep your balance.*
> *What does it mean that hope is as hollow as fear?*
> *Hope and fear are both phantoms*
> *that arise from thinking of the self.*
> *When we don't see the self as self,*
> *what do we have to fear?*

See the world as yourself.
Have faith in the way things are.
Love the world as yourself;
then you can care for all things.

"See the world as yourself," a perfect way to remember that we are all one. When something "bad" seems to be happening, I recall this passage from Isaiah 43:19: *"See, I am doing a new thing! Now it springs up; do you not perceive it? I am making a way in the wilderness and streams in the wasteland."*

The old is passing away. Sad, maybe. Scary, maybe. But don't resist. Allow the new to spring up because it is guaranteed to be better than before.

The most thrilling part to me is, "do you not perceive it?" It is almost a plea from the Universe: Please! Please! Please see what I am doing because I love you so much.

God turns bad things into blessings, but we have a vital part: we must see them right.

Seeing Things Right When They Seem So Wrong

In August 1996, I was diagnosed with HIV. I was very sick. At that time, the prognosis for people with the virus was poor. There was no real treatment, much less a cure. Yet by that point, I had already started down a spiritual path. I was concerned, of course, scared of the unknown, unsure about what was going to happen. But by some miracle, I did not panic or have a nervous breakdown.

I had gotten sober eighteen months earlier and was attending a variety of twelve-step meetings. Just after my diagnosis, I connected with another sober, HIV-positive man who was working with spiritual solutions for healing and wellness. He took me to events and retreats where healing was happening on a spiritual level.

Also, in clear evidence that I was being taken care of, the Universe had already put many supports in place for me. In April of that year, I quite unexpectedly started going to a church, when I was not looking for one. At Unity Church in Albany, New York, they talked about prosperity and physical healing—not in a dogmatic way, but in ways that rang bells, waking up the innate wisdom of the Universe inside of me.

Also in April 1996, I started seeing a therapist who helped me connect with my various inner children. He used various therapeutic techniques to heal old traumas so I could develop and strengthen my intuition. He also helped me connect with the angels all around us, higher-level beings that represent our best qualities and deepest spiritual powers.

And significantly, I was solidly in a career with excellent health coverage. Four years prior (when I could have been diagnosed, but chose not to be), I had none of these things in place. At that time, I was in no position to receive such news, so it clearly was kept from me until I was ready.

Instead of panicking, I used this seemingly terrible news to deepen my spiritual work—with some urgency and a stronger commitment than I might have had otherwise. I got a doctor and started on new medicines, which proved to be a miracle breakthrough.

Then, in early 1997, I saw a magazine ad for a company that bought life insurance policies. They'd give "dying" people a percentage of their policy's value. In turn, they got the full value upon death. Pretty gruesome: the sicker you are, the more they give you, betting you will die soon. They then collect a hefty profit on their investment.

I sold my policy, collecting almost 70 percent of its value. More than two decades later, I am still alive and well and healthy! Thank you, God.

The company went out of business. The receivership still sends me periodic postcards, checking to see if I'm still alive, waiting to recoup its (very bad) investment.

The point should be obvious: Was the HIV-positive diagnosis terrible news or good news? At the time, it seemed very bad, but in retrospect: "Terrible? Who knows?"

Through this process, I hope I am showing you that I practiced the spiritual principle of "seeing it right."

Not only did I collect a healthy settlement (pun intended), which enabled me to buy a house, travel, and enjoy life—all while getting healthier—but the "fatal" disease helped and encouraged me (forced me?) to deepen my spiritual practice. It lit a fire under me, motivating me to grow and change—to wake up!

Judging "not by appearances but by right judgment" is a powerful way to see and know things clearly from a higher and truer perspective.

Remember: Our job is not to *set* things right but to *see* things right.

Step 5—Admitted to God, to ourselves, and to another human being the exact nature of our wrongs.

In the twelve steps of recovery, Step 5 is about admitting our wrongs. This step can be intimidating, but it is a major step toward a new life, free from the old, dead past that has been holding us back.

What makes many people pause is admitting the "exact nature of our wrongs" to another person. We may think we have already admitted these things to ourselves, and we probably believe God already knows everything, but tell another person? That's asking too much.

The truth is we can fool ourselves into thinking we have made our peace with the Creative Power of the Universe and with ourselves. We can tell ourselves we have let go of these things from the past that trouble us and affect our mood, our sleep, our choices, and our lives. But in fooling ourselves, we stay stuck in the past. These events, fears, and resentments stay with us. Sharing them with another person requires courage, willpower, and "right judgment."

This step will free us once and for all from the weight of the past. Like an eagle trying to soar with 500 pounds tied around its leg, we have to cut the cord and let the dead past fall away. We must commit to doing Step 5 thoroughly, honestly, and completely, withholding nothing.

The second major consideration is whom do we do our fifth step with?

This choice must be made thoughtfully, with care. If we are in twelve-step recovery, our sponsor is a logical choice. If we belong to a church, synagogue, mosque, temple, or other house of worship, we could talk to our priest, rabbi, imam, or other faith leader.

Whomever we pick must be willing to listen without judgment and must be someone we trust to keep our confidences.

In practicing Steps 4 and 5, I felt a lot of shame, guilt, remorse, and fear. Fortunately, the Universe placed Jim F. in my life. He was the perfect person with whom to share. And I told him everything. He sat and listened, only interrupting to say, "Yeah, me too." Really? They told me if a behavior or wrongdoing has a name, it has been done before. I am not unique.

Once finished, we ceremoniously burned my 4th Step journal with all I had written. I left and went to a beautiful spot overlooking a great valley in Upstate New York. There I felt a 500-pound yoke lift right up off me.

I felt free! I felt like an adult for the first time in my life. I had done something courageous, liberating, and difficult—and I succeeded.

In *The Big Book* there are "promises" after Step 5:

> We pocket our pride and go to it, illuminating every twist of character, every dark cranny of the past. Once we have taken this step, withholding nothing, we are delighted. We can look the world in the eye. We can be alone at perfect peace and ease. Our fears fall from us. We begin to feel the nearness of our Creator. We may have had certain spiritual beliefs, but now we begin to have a spiritual experience. The feeling that the drink problem has disappeared will often come strongly. We feel we are on the Broad Highway, walking hand in hand with the Spirit of the Universe.

I encourage you to find a trusted friend, mentor, spiritual leader, or even a stranger and share your Step 4 with them. The rewards are beyond your wildest imagination, and they pay dividends for a lifetime.

Forgiveness

Steps four and five entail some serious housecleaning. We rid ourselves of a lifetime of garbage and debris that cluttered up our lives, weighed us down, and held us back. It kept us stuck in old thought patterns that got us nowhere.

Afterward, powerful forces will begin to awaken. One of many gifts you will begin receiving you will use with growing confidence, assurance, and power: the joy, the gift, the power of forgiveness.

Forgiveness will be discussed more in upcoming weeks, but for now, understand that it is a powerful healing force.

Prosperity depends upon releasing old, useless ideas to make room for fresh, new truthful ideas that work to manifest our heart's desires in all areas. If you have completed a thorough, searching, and fearless Step 4 and Step 5, the need for forgiveness should be obvious. Thoughts of blame, shame, guilt, remorse, anger, resentment, fear, lack, unworthiness, or other negative beliefs can be washed away in the light and spirit of forgiveness.

Forgiveness has been studied and debated for centuries, yet it is simple:

> We "Give +For." We give (love) for [blank].
>
> For+Give = Give For.
>
> In exchange for a hurt or slight, we give love.
>
> In exchange for a mistake, we give love.
>
> In exchange for a wrong done to us, we give love.
>
> In exchange for something we have done, for a poor choice we've made, we give love to ourselves.
>
> In exchange for a real or perceived injury, we give love.
>
> In exchange for times we have hurt others, we give ourselves love.
>
> In exchange for times we have been thoughtless or rude, we give ourselves love.
>
> In exchange for times we wish we had done or not done something, we give ourselves love.

The practice of forgiveness is powerful. It is a miraculous healing power. Forgiveness will make right what is wrong. In the light of Step 5, it is vital to bring forgiveness to bear on the situations we are releasing—for others, but especially for ourselves. Beating ourselves up doesn't do anyone any good. Let the past rest in peace and move forward, free, with a clean slate.

You have so many good things to look forward to!

ACTION ITEMS
Practice Lesson 108 from *A Course in Miracles*

This brief meditation is designed to awaken our awareness, to move us from separation to an awareness of the oneness of everything.

Please know that you are making a major shift in your thinking—and in the thinking of the world, literally saving the world from thousands of years of darkness and misery. You cannot overstate how important it is to move your mind away from the world's ideas to ground yourself solidly in God's ideas.

The meditation is:

> To give and to receive are one in truth.
>
> I will receive what I am giving now.
>
> Then close your eyes, and for five minutes, think of what you would hold out to everyone, to make it yours. You might, for instance, say:
>
> To everyone, I offer quietness.
>
> To everyone, I offer peace of mind.
>
> To everyone, I offer gentleness.
>
> Say each one slowly and then pause a while, expecting to receive the gift you gave. And it will come to you to the extent you gave it. You will find you have an equal return—that is what you asked for.
>
> It might also be helpful to think of one person to give your gifts to. They represent the others, and through them, you give to all.

Do Step 5

Find someone trustworthy to share your 5th Step. Choose carefully, but don't delay. Delay can prove to be a serious setback.

If you have written a thorough 4th Step, you have collected all the smelly garbage from your past in one place. Now bag it up and place it on the curb, to be removed from your life forever. Don't leave it sitting in your psychic space one second longer than necessary.

Free yourself from the past—Now! in the present—so your future can be new and different, better and fuller—full of all the good the Universe has in store for you.

Create the space necessary so your good can flow in.

Reread Week 5 at Least Twice

> ***Tithe***—*Divine Love, flowing through me, blesses and multiplies all that I have, all that I give and all that*

I receive. We are blessed to know that Spirit is our Source. God bless! Thank you, God!

Sing

"I Am So Blessed"
by Karen Drucker

I Am so blessed
I Am so blessed
I Am so grateful, for all that I have
I Am so blessed, I Am so blessed
I Am so grateful, I Am so blessed

We are so blessed
We are so blessed
We are so grateful, for all that we have
We are so blessed, We are so blessed
We are so grateful, We are so blessed

God bless! Thank you, God!

Week 6

The Power of Gratitude and Prayer

> *The path to heaven doesn't lie down in flat miles.*
> *It's in the imagination with which*
> *you perceive this world, and the*
> *gestures with which you honor it.*
> — Mary Oliver, "The Swan"

Prayer

Now it is time to add an important tool to help deepen our awareness. To manifest a prosperous life, happy, joyous, and free, as a spiritual being inhabiting physical reality, we need to understand prayer.

Prayer is misunderstood and misused by many people. Before we say what prayer is not, I want to give you my definition of what a prayer is:

> A prayer is the mental, emotional, physical, psychic, and spiritual energy that flows from us—consciously or unconsciously—which connects us to our Source, to manifest our world, our life, and our experience.

Prayer is *not* the mumbled words we say when we awake in the morning or before we go to bed at night.

Prayer is *not* the hasty plea we make when we're in trouble, the so-called "foxhole prayer."

Prayer is *not* the words we say automatically, without feeling or awareness, as a child might say grace before dinner.

We have been told that these are prayers, but while words are part of prayer, words alone do not make a prayer.

A little background first: We are highly creative beings, made by our Creator in the very same image and likeness as the Creative Force of the Universe. We have all of the attributes of our Creator.

A drop of sea water is not the ocean, yet within each drop are all the elements of the ocean. The drop is affected by the moon's pull just like its ocean-source. It is made up of the same chemical and molecular components as its source.

We are like that drop of sea water—infused with exactly the same qualities and elements as our Source. It is a well-known fact that our physical bodies are made up of 60 percent water, and our brains and hearts are made up of almost 75 percent water.

The Truth Is: We are in the ocean, and the ocean is in us.

In an earlier lesson, we also learned we are physically made of "star stuff." Matter, like oxygen and carbon, forged in the heat of billions of stars, created all we see.

The Truth Is: Spiritually, we are made of Universal Substance. We are made directly from the substance that is the Creative Intelligence of the Universe.

And like our Creator, we are also powerfully creative.

The Truth Is: We cannot help but create. We are creating all the time. We create without ceasing.

Therefore, *A Course in Miracles* warns us that there are no idle thoughts. All thinking produces form at some level. One lesson reminds us of this:

Lesson 16: I Have No Neutral Thoughts

> *There is no more self-contradictory concept than that of idle thoughts.* **What gives rise to the perception of a whole world can hardly be called idle.** *Every thought you have contributes to truth or to illusion; either it extends the truth, or it multiplies illusions.*
> *(Emphasis added.)*

Yes! Our thoughts "give rise to the perception of the whole world." Think about that. You create your world with your thoughts. What you think you see, you see. The question is:

What are we creating, and how are we creating it?

Powerful prayer aligns many elements:

- Our thoughts
- Our feelings
- Our beliefs
- Our words, which we think and say aloud
- Our actions, which we do
- Our hopes and dreams
- Our ideas

All these things combine in you to create your world.

The Truth Is: *A real, powerful, conscious prayer integrates everything you think, say, do, feel, and believe.*

So....

- A real prayer
- A true prayer
- A prayer that brings positive results
- A prayer that forms and shapes your world and your life

Is one in which all these inner elements are in harmony. Clearly, when these elements are in conflict (as they often are), our thinking is conflicted, our lives are conflicted, and so, our results are conflicted. Our prayer is conflicted, so it brings us results we do not want, or perhaps no results at all.

St. Paul said it wonderfully in Romans 7:14-17:

> So, the trouble is not with the law, for it is spiritual and good. The trouble is with me, for I am all too human.... I don't really understand myself, for I want to do what is right, but I don't do it. Instead, I do what I hate. But if I know that what I am doing is wrong, this shows that I agree that the law is good. So, I am not the one doing wrong; it is [my mistaken beliefs] living in me that does it.

In other words, the law—the spiritual principles—is not skewed. It's our thinking.

Incidentally, most English translations have St. Paul using the word "sin" in the last sentence. Take out the loaded word sin and translate it more accurately as: We "miss the mark"—due to our human thinking and our old, faulty beliefs.

Many people experience this phenomenon. They say, "I need to quit…" (drinking, overeating, smoking, being lazy, procrastinating, arguing, etc.). But they still do the thing they hate doing. Why?

We say we need to lose weight, but our weight stays the same or even increases. Why?

We say, "I'm going to fulfill my dream to [whatever your dream is]," and yet, it doesn't happen. Why?

Saying one thing but doing another, thinking one thing but subconsciously believing the opposite, hoping for this but feeling that—we can all recognize this maddening contradiction.

If our creative energies don't line up—if they are conflicted, different, or jumbled—our prayer is jumbled. Thoughts, words, beliefs, feelings, and actions not in alignment is not a recipe for successful living. Like a team rowing a boat, if everyone is rowing in different directions, the boat won't go anywhere…and it may even sink.

The Truth Is: Our head, heart, gut, thoughts, words, beliefs, and deeds must align with clarity and integrity. Then our prayer will be effective and powerful and will produce desirable results.

Begging, Bargaining, and Beseeching

We often misunderstand how to pray and what to pray for.

Traditionally, prayer has often meant begging, beseeching, and bargaining with God for something. We have been taught to see prayer as a way to get or avoid something.

Whining, pleading, bargaining, trading, and negotiating with the Universe, trying to get God to do something (or not do something), grant us something, stop something, or otherwise fulfill a wish list (much like a child has a Christmas list for Santa) is ineffective prayer.

This way of "praying" is based on a serious misconception: that God is changeable. It assumes that the Universe plays favorites.

Do we really believe that the Great Spirit says, "Yes" or "No" depending on how It feels today? Do we think we are granted grace and mercy based on whether we've been good or not? Or do we assume God just rolls dice, and everything is based on random and uncertain chance?

These are very old, very wrong, and unfortunately, very normal ways of praying.

The Universe does not operate in random or haphazard ways. Its laws are rational and orderly. In fact, one shorthand for GOD is Good Orderly Direction. Once we know God's immutable laws, we can apply them to get positive results.

We may think we do not believe this, but then we act and pray as if these things were true of God, which they are not.

James 1:17 says: "Every good and perfect gift is from above, coming down from the Father of the heavenly lights, *who does not change like shifting shadows.*" (Emphasis added.)

We All Deserve (and Receive) Blessings

> *"For he makes his sun rise on the evil and on the good,*
> *and sends rain on the just and on the unjust."*
> — Matthew 5:45

This verse simply means blessings are constantly being poured out upon everyone, regardless of who they are or what they do. Good and not-so-good people receive blessings in equal measure.

Huh? What's up with that? Why then does it seem like some people receive more than others? Remember: Do not judge by appearances. Someone who appears to have it all may be very unhappy. We cannot judge by material wealth or by the outer mask someone displays. We don't know what goes on inside someone's home, behind closed doors, and we certainly cannot know what goes on inside someone's heart.

A person who puts their faith in lack and limitation, in greed or other negative beliefs, may be monetarily very wealthy, yet be poor in spirit. They may have no peace of mind, no gratitude, no joy. Their thoughts put them outside the flow of Universal Good.

Their thoughts will cause them to miss the blessings constantly being poured out upon them.

A person who puts their faith in God, in good, in life, in generosity, in kindness, in compassion, and in other positive truths may be monetarily poor, yet they are rich in the kind of treasure that "does not rust."

> *"Do not store up for yourselves treasures on earth, where moth and rust destroy, and where thieves break in and steal. But store up for yourselves treasures in heaven, where moth and rust do not destroy, and where thieves do not break in and steal."*
> — Matthew 6:19-20

The valuable gifts that make us prosperous are the gifts of the Spirit: humility, serenity, health, wholeness, happiness, contentment, peace of mind, joy, life, wisdom, discernment, and Love.

These are the gifts we continually receive if we keep on giving. We receive these gifts from God, regardless of what we do, just by being a child of God, at one with the Universe. These gifts are always available—but we may block them with thoughts of lack and poverty. If so, we will be unaware of these gifts, even though God gives them to us unceasingly. Those who are open and ready to receive the gifts of the Spirit perceive blessings that flow from Source, and they can receive them consciously.

Being "Good" Is Not a Requirement

> *"And Jesus said to him, 'Why do you call me good? No one is good except God alone.'"*
> — Mark 10:18

Jesus tells the "rich, young man" in the parable that nobody is good, not even Jesus himself; only God is good. Wow! If even Jesus is "not good"—and he is our best human example of a conscious and clear connection to Source—then we who are also "not good" can rest assured that we too receive all the good God can supply.

But when one's focus is on lack, greed, dishonesty, selfishness, or other negative ideas, they cannot easily see the blessings coming their way. When we focus on what we are "losing," we may never notice what is being made new. Judging by appearances, we focus on what is being done *to* us and completely miss the good coming through *for* us.

Prayer Is

To sum up, effective prayer integrates all of what we think, feel, say, believe, and know with what we do. When all is aligned, our prayer is powerful, connecting us to the Creative Source. Universal Presence responds to our prayer and the results manifest.

The activating words connecting us to Spirit are "I am." Remember "I Am That I Am" from Week 3, when Moses asked God what His name was? Here is a part of the story many people miss. When Moses asks God, "Who shall I say sent me?" (What is Your name? or What is Your way?), he is asking God a trick question.

In that culture, names were not random. They meant something. A name was a sign of the person's greatest attribute, or a plant or animal's most telling feature or its greatest strength. Moses is asking God to say something important about Himself. What is it about you that really matters? What makes you tick?

God's answer is I exist. I Am. I Am That I Am. I Be. I Am is the rock, the foundation of God, of Spirit—and of us. Whatever we say after "I am" declares our truth, telling God, the Universe, and our deepest self what we believe is true for us. This is our prayer—whatever we say, feel, and believe after we say, "I am."

The Truth Is: Be aware of what comes after "I am" and never use the phrase in vain.

Let's close this section on prayer with a quote from Myrtle Fillmore, co-founder of the Unity Church with her husband, Charles Fillmore.

Myrtle's story is fascinating. She discovered the Truth Movement in the mid-1800s in the United States, and she used these "Truth Ideas" to heal her sickly and weak body. She attended lectures on practical use of spiritual principles. She learned how these principles could infuse life, health, awareness, peace, and power into her mind and body—and into her life.

These principles healed Myrtle physically, and she and Charles used them to help others. From humble beginnings in Kansas City, Unity Church has become a worldwide fellowship, bringing light to millions.

Myrtle writes in one of her letters:

> We have a very decided part; we are to cease worrying, and being anxious, and thinking and speaking of the past and of the apparent lack and idleness. We are to concentrate all our attention upon the Truth of God, and the truth of our own being, upon the very things we would see taking place in our life. We cannot do this so long as we have negative thoughts in our heart.
>
> As we pray, the word of life is going down into us, breaking up old fixed beliefs and reorganizing our life. The word of life—life as God has planned it—is taking hold of our subconsciousness, and we know that we are free and will begin to use our freedom. Working in the consciousness of freedom, we will be happy and well and busy and prosperous. But our attention will be upon what we are doing rather than upon outer results. The results will take care of themselves once we have started our foundation in Truth.
>
> "With God all things are possible. Those who receive spiritual help are the ones who place their undivided faith in God and who bring their thinking in line with His Truth. Ye shall know the truth, and the truth shall make you free." (Myrtle Fillmore, "Our Part in Prayer" in *Healing Letters*, p. 33-35)

Gratitude!

In earlier weeks, we introduced denials to break up old fixed beliefs. A denial is followed with a positive affirmation to fill the void with a thought more aligned with the good orderly direction (GOD) of the Universe.

Now we add a third element: gratitude. Some people say gratitude is the most powerful way to align our thinking with God's mind.

Feeling gratitude, we can make gratitude a verb and take action. Even more powerfully, we can simply be grateful.

"Thank you," can be a powerful and effective prayer. Deny what's false and affirm what is true. Then add an "attitude of gratitude" to put a higher energy into the mix.

When you give a gift, how do you feel if the person barely acknowledges you? You probably won't give that person another gift anytime soon. God doesn't need your gratitude, but you need the energy and vitality that comes from feeling thankful.

Having gratitude:

- Shows appreciation for what is being given
- Shows the Universe we recognize it as our Source
- Shows we don't take things for granted
- Generates energies of joy and love
- Acknowledges that we have a real sense of being cared for and loved.
- Awakens in us an awareness that we, too, need to give. We must reciprocate.
- Reminds us we are indebted to others (in a healthy way).
- Causes us to be aware of the interconnectedness of all beings.
- Causes us to recognize other people as important.
- Awakens us to the connection between gratitude, compassion, and wisdom.

Buddhists talk about boundless kindness, boundless compassion, boundless joy, and boundless equanimity. These all flow from gratitude. However, you can go even deeper, even more powerfully, into gratitude.

Gratitude in the Midst of the Storm

When things go well, gratitude is easy. But when bad news and events throw us off balance, when something happens that is not to our liking, when we encounter difficulties or tragedies, do we have gratitude then, in the midst of hardships and under these circumstances? Not likely, not easily, certainly not automatically or immediately. Almost nobody would.

Bad news from the doctor, a job loss, a divorce, a flat tire, or worse…these things bring about common emotions—fear, anger, sadness, confusion, depression, rage, etc.—which can easily compel us to a range of responses: self-pity, resentment, control, violence, withdrawal, lethargy, frantic action, panic, etc.

But:

- We can stop and have a new thought that is true in Spirit.
- We can stop, remembering that the Universe is benevolent.
- We can cultivate our pronoia, remembering that all things conspire for our good.
- We can choose to look past appearances, pausing in the moment to "see it right."

Easing ourselves into a new way of thinking, we will *always* find the silver lining in the dark cloud.

The Truth Is: Serenity is not the absence of a storm but calm in the midst of a storm.

Serene in the face of adversity, we remember that we have spiritual tools. Divine assistance is ready to help when we do our "decided part" and "see it right!"

It's All for You!

Romans 8:28 says: "Everything works together for good for those who love God and are called according to his purpose."

The key word there is *everything*. All things work in our favor, and for the good of all concerned, when we see it right! In some Neo-Pagan and Wiccan practices, the proper way to end a prayer is to say: "For the Good of All, according to the free will of all, and so it must be."

This phrase allows us to pray for someone, or for some outcome, while considering we know but a little. Spirit knows what is best for all concerned. Only Spirit can bring *everything* into alignment for the good of all concerned. Our prayer can never be a "win or lose" proposition. It must be for the highest good of all. Our human minds cannot resolve or "figure out" a way to make everything come out perfectly, for our good and for the good of everyone.

Only God can see the bigger picture and fashion a solution that benefits all. Prayer "turns it over," acknowledging our limited understanding, so the Universe can resolve things in a way that meets everyone's needs.

Many people end a prayer with this phrase, "This, or something better. Thank you, God." In that way, we offer our best idea of a solution, allowing that God knows what is needed better than we ever could.

An AA book about Step 2 is called, *Came to Believe*. In it is a section that changed my life and propelled me along the path of recovery when I was faltering and in danger of quitting. The section is called, "God is Good" and the author states: "I have developed an enormous faith in God. He is good. My understanding is that *everything* He sends my way is for my benefit" ("Came to Believe," p. 86-87).

The writer realized that everything that came into his life was for his highest and best good, and the word "everything" is in italics to emphasize everything.

Appearances are powerful illusions. But no matter how tragic things can be, Spirit can turn them around to become blessings, if we *pronoically* believe in the complete goodness of the Universe and we strive to see it right.

Finally, perhaps most importantly, gratitude should not be just a feeling. It must be an action verb. Gratitude that will move Heaven and Earth requires action. Show your gratitude to others, to yourself, and to God. Turn that feeling into a force that generates more good—and more gratitude—in your life and in the world.

Take action. Express gratitude. Demonstrate gratitude. Live gratitude. Embody gratitude every day in every way you can.

Don't try to set things right, but see things right by using gratitude. It will help you to look past appearances, past what seems to be lacking, to show you what is coming through, new, better, exciting, and alive.

Step 6—Became entirely ready to have God remove all these character defects.

A review of the first six steps of our twelve-step process could be summarized as follows:

1. We admitted we had a problem in Step 1.
2. We admitted our problem was largely of our own making because our thinking was warped in Step 2.
3. We decided we needed to turn our thinking, our feeling, and actions over to a Higher Power, which knows better and is infinitely good in Step 3.
4. We looked over our thinking and determined what was old, tired, ineffective, or even harmful. And we examined the garbage of our interior life and the problems it caused us in Step 4.
5. We examined what we found with God and another human being—and gathered all the garbage up—in Step 5.

Now, in Step 6, we take the stinky, smelly, nasty garbage we've collected and cart it to the curb. It has clogged up the flow of our good long enough.

In Step 6, we call our spiritual trash collector to come pick up the garbage. We cannot remove our own character defects—our troublesome thinking and personality traits. God will do it for us.

For most, this is a lifelong process; rarely does someone get hit by a lightning bolt. Most have a slow process, where the worst of their issues are addressed first. Our awakening awareness knows too much now so we cannot ignore these issues or try to fool ourselves by saying, "They're not that bad."

Often when a character defect is ready to be removed, it first grows so out of control that we can see unmistakably, in clear light, how dysfunctional it is.

We want it gone. It no longer serves us. That is how quitting smoking happened for me in 1998. I smoked for more than twenty-five years, but after being diagnosed with HIV, I knew I ought to quit, but I "just couldn't." I tried and tried and tried, and I relapsed dozens of times.

Then, my smoking flew out of control. I smoked more than ever. When I managed to quit for a few days, I ended up smoking even more when I relapsed. During my last attempt, after a particularly long stretch without cigarettes, I decided I could smoke one cigarette a week. Insanity for a nicotine addict.

But I was successful...for two weeks. Then I had my cigarette for the week on Wednesday, and my cigarette for next week on Thursday. Within hours, I had bought a pack and smoked three or four cigarettes one after the other. I was so angry (and a bit sick). I crushed and threw the pack away, and I haven't had another cigarette since.

The *Tao Te Ching* writer, Lao Tsu, understood this process. In Chapter 36, he writes:

> If you want to shrink something,
> you must first allow it to expand.
> If you want to get rid of something,
> you must first allow it to flourish.
> If you want to take something,
> you must first allow it to be given.
> This is called the subtle perception
> of the way things are.
> The soft overcomes the hard.
> The slow overcomes the fast.
> Let your workings remain a mystery.
> Just show people the results.

The great mystical poet William Blake knew this when he wrote these lines in *The Marriage of Heaven and Hell*:

> *The road of excess*
> *Leads to the palace of wisdom.*

Watch for character defects to flare up: anger, chronic sadness, procrastination, self-pity, dishonesty, etc. When we live life unconsciously, it can seem like we're just having a bad day. But when we are consciously aware, we notice our defects. Even if we are not able to stop them, we notice the pain they cause us. We are becoming "entirely ready" to have God remove this problem that is clogging up our good.

Instead of being dismayed, you can revel in the fact that you are making good progress. You are on the right path. Whatever your character defects, the good news is that the worst will go first.

You have a part in all of this, though; you have to make yourself entirely ready.

You made a searching, fearless, and thorough list of your defects and assets, and you went over them with another person. Now add the power of prayer to align your thoughts, beliefs, ideas, feelings, words, hopes, dreams, and actions in the same direction—a good orderly direction (GOD).

Look at your list of character defects and see what needs to be removed. Then, become entirely ready to have God remove them. The ones that flare up are the first to go.

ACTION ITEMS
Review the section on prayer

Examine your prayer life. How do you pray? Begin to see your denial and affirmation statements as prayers. They are much more than just memorized words. They need to be aligned with feelings, beliefs, ideas, thoughts, actions, and more. Put your whole body into them. Put all your senses into them. See, feel, touch, taste, and hear them. Use images, imagination, and belief.

Pay attention

What do you say and/or think after "I am"? Don't be discouraged or beat tourself up. Simply noticing when you say something negative after "I am" is half the battle. Just notice and adjust, vowing to do better.

How do you pray?

Remember, we are always praying. Does your mind turn toward the wisdom within? Do you beg, bargain with, or beseech God? Do you say one thing but do another? Are your various parts aligned—head, heart, and guts?

Practice Deeper Gratitude

Practice an "attitude of gratitude," not just for the good things that come your way, but for *everything* that comes your way. The good and not so good—all are here to help you wake up and grow, *if* you see them right.

Gratitude is the third leg of the triangle, along with denials and affirmations.

Examine how your gratitude manifests? Is it just a feeling? Do you make gratitude an action, a verb?

Write Regular Gratitude Lists

Put gratitude into action. Find ways to feel and show your joy. Find ways to feel and believe that uncomfortable or difficult situations deserve gratitude, too.

Once, in a very dark time, I forced myself to write a 100-item gratitude list. Use your prosperity journal to make daily gratitude lists. They don't have to be 100 items, but you can find at least ten things a day to be grateful for.

Review Your Goal for the Course

This is your one goal for the course in light of the ideas about prayer and gratitude.

Do Step 6

This is a vital step. Alcoholics Anonymous literature states that Step 6, "separates the men from the boys." (Apologies for the archaic language.) Why? Because we may feel we have done enough by doing a searching inventory and sharing it with another. Who needs or wants to do more than that?

Also, the previous steps are clear and concrete in their actions, while this step may seem vague. There seems to be not so much to do here. Yet there is a lot of inner soul-searching combined with becoming aware of our outer attitudes and behaviors, noticing them and changing course. This is what it means to become "entirely ready."

Another impediment could be that you may deny you even *have* character defects. Or you may deny your attitudes and behaviors are destructive or troublesome. After all, they seem to protect you from people, places, and situations that seem to threaten you. Besides, do you have to be perfect?

But to halt halfway through the steps would be a shame. Likely these defects are not horrible (for example, we may be greedy, but not enough to rob banks; we may be angry, but not enough to assault someone). But even in their milder forms, they cause us—and the people around us—trouble, misery, and pain. To have the joyously abundant life we deserve, we need to make ourselves ready for these defects to be removed.

Look at your list of character assets and defects. What defects would you like to have removed first? What defect *needs* to be removed because it is causing you so much trouble and pain? Let the Universe show you which one is ripe for picking. Pick it, and do whatever is necessary to become "entirely ready."

Reread Week 6 at Least Twice

> ***Tithe****—Divine Love, flowing through me, blesses and multiplies all that I have, all that I give and all that I receive. We are blessed to know that Spirit is our Source. God bless! Thank you, God!*

Sing

"I Am So Blessed"
by Karen Drucker

I Am so blessed
I Am so blessed
I Am so grateful, for all that I have
I Am so blessed, I Am so blessed
I Am so grateful, I Am so blessed

We are so blessed
We are so blessed
We are so grateful, for all that we have
We are so blessed, We are so blessed
We are so grateful, We are so blessed

God bless! Thank you, God!

Week 7

Imagination: Putting Wings on Your Dreams

*Alice laughed. "There's no use trying," she said.
"One can't believe impossible things."
"I daresay you haven't had much practice,"
said the Queen.
"When I was your age, I always did it for
half-an-hour a day.
Why, sometimes I've believed as many as
six impossible things before breakfast."*
— Lewis Carroll, *Alice's Adventures in Wonderland*

Imagination

In Week 6, we talked about prayer—aligning our thinking, feeling, words, beliefs, etc. to make a powerful prayer that works. We want to put all our being into our prayer: thoughts, feelings, words, beliefs, and actions.

Denials, affirmations, and gratitude are prayers—powerful, effective ways to pray and break up old thinking, canceling out outdated beliefs, to replace them with spiritual laws, truths that work.

This week we will tie them all together using another mind power. Of course you already use this power, but not fully or consistently. When used to its fullest extent, this powerful engine lets you consciously see positive, successful outcomes before they manifest in physical reality.

This is the power of Imagination.

Absolutely nothing can be created or achieved unless it is first imagined. Imagination creates three-dimensional pictures of our beliefs. Then faith is activated, driving the creative spirit of the Universe like an engine that drives everything you see, everything that ever was or ever will be. Full use of imagination shifts your consciousness away from scattered, ineffective thinking, to focused, intentional, conscious, clear, and specific thinking.

In *Prosperity Plus*, Mary Morrissey said, "Everything is always created twice." Once in imagination and then in manifestation.

A full imagination involves much more than words. To powerfully manifest your good, your words plus sight, sound, taste, touch, and smell all need to be marshaled.

Using *all* your senses creates a powerful image, a three-dimensional, holographic, and sensory landscape in which to build a goal, a project, an event, or a path.

Try this exercise:

Set your twelve-week goal firmly in your mind. You have already posted it in places where you can see it consciously and unconsciously.

Now, expand upon the idea. Visualize the process to go from here to there.

Let's use an example I particularly like:

If my goal is a vacation in the south of France, I first see myself getting my ticket. See yourself getting *your* ticket.

Maybe you go online or to a travel agent. Visualize the ticket in your hands. How does it feel? What does it look like? Is it a paper ticket? An electronic ticket on your phone? What does it say? What seat did you choose? Is it first class, business class, economy plus? Notice the airline name, your name, and the travel dates.

Now visualize yourself in the busy, bustling airport. It's the day of your flight. Hear the airport sounds: people talking, planes taking off, announcements on the public address system. See the people sitting at the gate. See the big windows that look out onto the runways. See the planes standing in a row at the gates while the workers load baggage or refuel the planes.

Hear the boarding call for your flight. See yourself in line to board. Your ticket is scanned, and you walk down the gangway to board the plane. See the cabin stewards greet you as you enter the plane along with your fellow passengers.

Feel the excitement. You're on your way!

Feel the comfortable seat. In my visualization, I pick a first-class seat. It has rows of only two people, and there is plenty of extra leg room. I see my two little dogs with me, comfortable in their carrier, as I always travel with them. I visualize that the airline has accommodated the dogs easily and without any hassle whatsoever.

I feel the plane take off and enjoy the meals and in-flight movies. I nap and wake up just in time to see our plane on its final approach. I see the beach below and the azure blue waters of the Mediterranean Sea. I see the bright sun and blue sky.

Now visualize the drive to the hotel from the airport. Did you rent a car? Take an airport shuttle? Whatever. See yourself arriving at the hotel and checking in. You can see the beach right across the street. Talk to the front desk people. In my visualization, I have booked a king suite on a lower floor.

Hear the whirling elevator as you ascend to your room. Use the key to open the door. What a magnificent room and a stunning view. Thank you, God! You have arrived safely and are ready to enjoy the Riviera.

We just took ourselves from wherever we are sitting to the Côte d'Azur. And yet we never left our comfort zone couch. We used the powerful tool that is our imagination. Visualization, using all our senses, got us there in our mind's eye.

Later, we will discuss a technique that takes this process to an even higher level—and gives it wings. But before we do, we need a quick detour to help us distinguish between correctly using imagination and the misuse of our creative mind through fantasy.

Fantasy vs. Imagination

Fantasy takes our God-given imagination—the ability to create our lives using spiritual laws and tools—and squanders it by conjuring up unbelievable or destructive scenarios that are possibly harmful to ourselves and others.

I am not referring to science fiction and fantasy, which use imagination in literature for entertainment and enlightenment, envisioning possible futures for humankind.

Fantasy that misuses our creativity and imagination is like putting a big, fancy car (our beautiful imagination) in a ditch—spin those wheels as fast as you want, you will go nowhere.

Spending hours, days, weeks, or a lifetime in fantasy or daydreaming may be pleasurable, but it is highly unproductive and can even turn from a habit into an obsession.

In negative fantasy—aka worry—we entertain our worst fears, projecting future situations we "know" will turn out badly or ruminating over old traumas and hurts of long ago from people who may not even be around anymore.

Time and energy focused on negative moments from the past or melancholy reminiscing about good times gone by misuses our creative gift of imagination.

Similarly, by projecting bad outcomes about the future, fearing and dreading things that may never happen, or going into flights of fancy about scenarios we could or should never achieve, we use our imagination wrongly.

How Does This Work Out Better Than I Could Possibly Imagine?

This question comes from a talk given by Mark Shepard, prolific writer of powerful and moving spiritual songs and chants. He suggests we ask the question and then sit with it and do not seek an answer.

I have incorporated this question into my workshop, "Healing Through Illness" that I do for people who face sickness and other physical problems. The question is powerful for physical healing because it opens our minds, connecting our thinking to our higher self, the innate wisdom of the Universe that resides in us.

Any troubling situation inherently carries the seeds of a gift. I pointed out earlier that we tend automatically to focus on the difficulty. It takes effort to look past the tragedy to see the miracles and gifts arising out of the problem. It's natural to mourn a life that is breaking down, things that are going away. But then we miss what God is doing for us that is new and better.

Inherent in Shepard's question are the seeds of the answer: This (situation/problem/difficulty/trouble/sadness) is not only going to work itself out, but it is going to work out better than I could possibly imagine. What a promise! What a gift!

The question is a direct portal to pronoia. Asking it, we will realize that life, God, troubles, difficulties are not here to hurt us. They are here to help us heal, to give us gifts. We need to see them to accept them, and get the healing they offer.

When we ask, "How does this work out better than I could possibly imagine?" we are declaring "This is going to work out, and despite any worry or fear, it is going to work out in a way beyond my wildest imagination, for my good and the good of all concerned."

In that mindset, you know you have a powerful, loving partner (God). You can turn your mind from negative imagination (aka, fantasy or worry) to positive imagination that brings positive results. With this in mind, you are ready to…

Put Wings to Your Dreams

Imagination used rightly brings results. Envisioning future actions puts wings to your dreams and prayers. Putting wings to your prayers ensures you are not merely daydreaming or fantasizing. Turning a dream that truly reflects your heart's desire into reality requires the conscious use of imagination plus action.

What to do first? What step can I take now to make my dream come true? The Tao says,

> "The journey of a thousand miles
> starts with a single step."

If it is within my realm of believability, it will be mine.

The *Narcotics Anonymous* basic text says, "Growth is not the result of wishing but of action and prayer." As a formerly active alcoholic and drug addict, I spent countless hours fantasizing about what I would do, where I would go, what I would become, what I should have said, what I would have done, regretting things, saying, "if only," etc.

Meanwhile, nothing I hoped for ever happened. Broke, delusional, grandiose, and inebriated, I had big dreams while my life slowly sank into oblivion. I have a wonderful faculty of imagination, but I was not conscious of the process of turning away from wild fantasies to achievable, manageable goals.

Once, I saw an advertisement in a magazine for a sixteenth-century French farmhouse for sale. I wrote to the seller and they replied, sending me pictures and descriptions of the main house and the many buildings on the property. It was a fantasy! I was making minimum wage, and I was deeply in debt, smoking pot and cigarettes, drinking, and going nowhere. I *was* that car spinning my wheels furiously in the ditch.

Remember, as someone once said, "Never confuse movement with progress."

The dream of France was in my heart. There was nothing wrong with sending away for the brochure. Yet I could only fulfill my dream when I found a spiritual path and the spiritual tools offered here in *Prosperity Now!*, which bring results. Before then, all was idle nonsense.

Correct use of imagination is conscious and purposeful with awareness that higher forces are active in your life, always for your highest good. It also means doing the footwork, doing the next right thing, to put wings on your dreams, put wings on your prayers to "Begin it now!"

Once you begin, all manner of help and resources will spring up to meet you. Things you never envisioned, never would have known to ask for, will materialize. It is truly a miraculous process, and it is yours.

A story from just days before I began my recovery may help illustrate the power of this process.

How God Gave Me My Career

The stage was set for God to give me my dream career way back in 1977, when I was only nineteen. After having our first child, my girlfriend and I got married. We were poor; I was working as a dishwasher at a hotel in my small Upstate New York mill town. We managed to get enough wedding money to have a weekend honeymoon—in Albany, New York.

That weekend, for some reason, I decided I wanted to see the New York State Capitol. I was drawn to it. When we went downtown on a Saturday, it was closed tight, so we couldn't go in.

Flash forward fourteen years. I was heavily into my addictions but managed to finish a two-year associates degree. It only took ten years! By 1991, I had moved to Albany and was taking classes part-time at the State University of New York at Albany.

That spring, I saw a flier for internships in the New York state legislature. I went to the information session and was dismayed to read that one criterion was an age limit. The program was for people twenty-six or under. I was already over thirty, so the internship was not available to me—or so I thought.

Jump forward two more years. I was finishing up my bachelor's degree in English literature in the English honors program. I was doing much better. While not sober (yet), I was dabbling in twelve-step recovery, getting good grades, and becoming more interested in meditation and other spiritual matters.

On campus, I saw another flier for the assembly internship program, so I went to the informational meeting, even though I "knew" I was not eligible. At the meeting, I listened to the presentation and asked, "What about the age limit?"

"What age limit?" the presenter asked.

"Last time you had to be under twenty-six years old."

"We never had an age limit."

Huh?

I applied for the program and was accepted. When I got the news I had been accepted, I flew over to the campus office to pick up my orientation information packet. For some unknown reason, when I got there the university's liaison snarled at me and brusquely threw my packet on the counter.

Hmm.

On January 3, 1993, I became an assembly intern. I went through orientation and was assigned by the intern director to the most prestigious placement accepting interns that year: the counsel to the majority leader, Cindy Shenker. In her office, I saw the whole legislative process from the top of the ladder.

While other interns were going home on Thursdays, our office was just ramping up work to get ready for the next week's floor debates. I couldn't have been given a better assignment. That internship led to twenty-two years in the top levels of state government and politics.

Then came the kicker: Years later, I was in the office of Jim Murphy, the internship director. We had become friends and colleagues. We were discussing my intern class and recounting war stories. I told him about how I had got my packet and how the university liaison had been very rude to me.

"Oh," Jim said. "He was angry at me too. He sent your application over marked, 'Not Recommended,' and I overruled him. I looked at your application and something inside me said, 'I have to have John Frederick in this class.'"

Well, that mystery was solved and the forces that conspired (pronoia) to get me on this long-dreamed-of career path began to come into focus.

Because the first time I investigated the intern program, I was severely addicted, struggling to stay afloat financially, emotionally, spiritually, and physically, if I had applied then, I either would have been rejected or I would have been accepted and surely blown the opportunity.

But two years later, I was on the verge of sobriety, I was dabbling in twelve-step recovery, and God knew I was ready to succeed. God kept me from making a mistake in 1991, and so, somehow, I "saw" an age limit that wasn't there.

Then, on top of that miracle, Jim Murphy accepted my application over the university's objections.

Then, on top of that, he put me in the highest office that had an intern, one out of the mainstream of the normal intern experience. While other interns worked for individual assembly members, I worked for the top counsel to the majority leader.

The education I received in my internship turned into the lifetime career of my dreams, one I would never have had if I didn't "begin it now!"

Now I know why I wanted to see the capitol that dreary October afternoon on my honeymoon in glamorous Albany, New York. I was drawn to that historic and beautiful building because my soul knew I belonged there. Except in Paris, I have never felt more at home than when sitting and working in the massive assembly chamber with its historic character, lively debates, political drama, and legal and legislative importance.

God set the stage and dimmed the lights. I just had to show up and say my lines on cue.

Goals and the Far Horizon

We set a goal that is within our realm of believability, something we are clear and definite about. We do the inner work. We do the outer work. We act.

We conceive the goal. We believe the goal. And we take action to achieve the goal. Thank you, God!

Now what? Do we sit on our laurels and say, "That's it"?

Of course not.

Have goals in many different areas. Part of an abundant, vibrant, and exciting life is a multitude of ideas, goals, and possibilities stretching far into the future, as far as the eye can see—and beyond.

The limit of our sight is our horizon. We can walk all day and the horizon will be just the same distance away tomorrow, next month, and next year. We will never reach the horizon on Earth, and in human form, we will never reach our horizon in Spirit. We can move toward it, but it is an unobtainable place.

The horizon is like God, or the Tao. **Always keep your eyes on the horizon. Always keep your eyes on God.** Yet, as we approach our goals, reach them, and move past them, the ultimate goal will always be before us. We cannot approach it, but we can use its infinite power.

Tao Te Ching, Poem 14:

Look, and it can't be seen.
Listen, and it can't be heard.
Reach, and it can't be grasped. Above, it isn't bright.
Below, it isn't dark.
Seamless, unnamable,
it returns to the realm of nothing.
Form that includes all forms,
image without an image,
subtle, beyond all conception.
Approach it and there is no beginning;
follow it and there is no end.
You can't know it, but you can be it,
at ease in your own life.

> *Just realize where you come from:*
> *this is the essence of wisdom.*
> (Emphasis added)

Our goals will come and go. Some will be achieved, others won't. Some goals on our list will lose their importance, others will conflict, and we will have to choose.

Our goals are mileposts on the highway. We approach them, reach them, celebrate them, and move on. Our goals are important but are just a means to an end, not the end themselves.

Progress on goals builds our new life, using spiritual tools, mastering spiritual powers—powers that have been inside of us all along: honesty, faith, perseverance, trust, hope, love, zeal, patience, discernment, joy, willingness, open-mindedness, steadfastness, generosity, and more.

We are becoming a fully spiritual being inside a human experience.

A sole focus on our goals misses the meaning of our human journey: to be our highest self and to help others see and be their highest selves. Enjoy your goals, strive for them, but focus always on the limitless horizon.

Treasure Maps (Vision Boards)

An effective way to use your powerful imagination to create your life and your world is by using treasure maps. A good map takes us where we want to go. A good map is easily read and has clear signs, directions, and markers, showing us where something is and how to get there.

Treasure maps are a time-honored and proven technique for manifesting and creating *Prosperity Now!*—first in imagination and then in physical reality. Treasure maps are simply collages, pictures of whatever you seek. Images cut out from old magazines bring vague mental pictures to life. These physical images reinforce mental images, manifesting what we want.

A treasure map uses your imagination to embellish every detail. Details are important. What do things look like? What images give you feelings of contentment, fulfillment, love, and joy? What ideas, words, and phrases get your juices flowing? Put them in your treasure map. Be open-minded. It is a serendipitous process. Comb magazines for images that speak to you. You will find ideas and images that hadn't occurred to you before. Sometimes we don't know something until we see it, and we respond with a resounding, "Ah!"

Of course, obtaining earthly things can be wonderful. They are not bad in and of themselves. We all deserve nice things. But by themselves, things do not bring lasting happiness. And they certainly don't bring good health, a wealth of friends, or a deep and meaningful spiritual life.

For the real fruits of the spirit, you will want to create....

I Am Map

An "I Am Map" is a treasure map, but not for a specific thing. It's a treasure map that guides us toward a newer, higher state of being.

Focusing on ways to become a better person, exploring areas where we would like to improve, we are doing Step 6—becoming "entirely ready" to lose old, dysfunctional ways of thinking and acting.

Use your imagination to create an I Am Map, a collage of vibrant images, colorful pictures, words, and phrases that represent attributes you would like to acquire or strengthen.

Put your I Am Map in a place where you will see it regularly. It will consciously and unconsciously imbue your mind and heart with those traits, moving them into your subconscious where they will take root.

Characteristics such as being thoughtful, kind, compassionate, honest and forthright, courageous, trustworthy, generous, vivacious, responsible, frugal, dignified, patient, etc. can be cultivated.

When we move from making treasure maps (for things we want) to making I Am Maps for things we want *to be*, we move from acquiring things to acquiring a better personality, a better character, a higher state of being.

The world says if we *have* more then we can *do* more; then we will *be* more.

What the world believes is the opposite of what Spirit says.

The Truth Is: First we must *be* more; then we can *do* more, and then we will *have* more!

Real joy, happiness, and success lie in strengthening our spiritual, mental, emotional, and psychological faculties so we are more at ease and at peace, more aligned with the creative power of the Universe, which always works with us for our highest and best good.

Step 7—Humbly asked God to remove our shortcomings.

Step 6, you'll remember, said, "Became entirely ready to have God remove all these character defects."

Step 7 says, "Humbly asked God to remove our shortcomings."

In Step 6, we looked at the list of character defects and assets we compiled in Step 4 and discussed in Step 5. Doing so, we started the process of becoming "entirely ready" to have our defects removed by our Higher Power.

Character defects, dysfunctional or negative attributes, create conditions in our inner and outer lives that prevent us from living fully and serenely. They create problems for us and for others, causing turmoil and confusion, if not outright hostility and anger, or sadness, disappointment, and resentment. They slow us down, send us off track, poison our spirit, and destroy our hopes and dreams. Our character defects are like the bars of a prison. Our purpose here is not to study the bars, but to escape the prison.

Looking at your Step 4 list, certain items will make themselves known to you, usually the ones that cause the most pain. In my experience, character defects tend to flare up when they are ready to be removed.

Remember these lines from Week 6?

> *Tao Te Ching, Chapter 36*
> *If you want to shrink something,*
> *you must first allow it to expand.*
> *If you want to get rid of something,*
> *you must first allow it to flourish.*

When a character defect really shows up, it is a good sign. Awareness must come first. A good shorthand for this spiritual process of awakening is: Awareness, Acceptance, Action!

Awareness is everything. We are souls awakening to our brilliant magnificence, to our reality—we are powerful spiritual beings capable of amazing miracles.

The Truth Is: We are becoming aware.

Becoming aware of how we fall short lets us choose. We refuse to stay on a dead-end path. We can see clearly just how destructive and imprisoning our anger, self-pity, laziness, pride, lust, etc. are. These defects can ruin our lives.

Character Defects vs. Shortcomings

What is the difference between character defects and shortcomings? An example should make this clear. Am I impatient? Then my character defect is impatience. I am too impatient.

The shortcoming is I need more patience. I don't have enough patience.

Steps 6 and 7 shrink character defects and strengthen character assets.

We want *less* greed and *more* generosity. We want less selfishness and more selflessness. We want to be less lustful and more virtuous. Building character assets helps us be rid of character defects.

Step 7 requires the use of another spiritual tool to help us grow and prosper. That spiritual quality is:

Humility

"Humbly asked...." What is humility? And why do we want it?

Many people believe humility is synonymous with being passive, servile, or taking whatever crumbs might fall off the table.

It's not.

Nothing is further from the truth.

The Truth Is: Humility is truth. Humility is power. Humility is honesty.

Humility is no more than an honest appraisal of who and what you are—a Child of God. Humility is the essence of the Serenity Prayer:

> *God, grant me the serenity*
> *To accept the things I cannot change*
> *The courage to change the things I can*
> *And the wisdom to know the difference.*

Humble, we clearly know our place in the Universe and accept all we cannot change. Knowing we are powerless is humbling. The precious quality of humility lets us focus on those things we can change. If we don't know, we admit it so we can focus on learning. In humility, we are teachable, open-minded, and willing to learn.

St. Augustine said something like the *Tao Te Ching*, Poem 36 when he said:

> *Do you wish to rise?*
> *Begin by descending.*
> *You plan a tower that will pierce the clouds?*
> *Lay first the foundation of humility.*

Humility is a solid foundation for your new, prosperous life, free from fear and doubt and full of faith and power. With a proper perspective on your place in the Universe, you are free to choose new ways that will bring you further along your path and goals in any situation.

Plato wrote that Socrates was the wisest because he knew he knew nothing. Being humble, he was open-minded, willing to question, open to possibilities. If we think we know, then we are stuck in our certainty. We are a closed book, not open to new information. If we are shown we're wrong, we are likely to pull out the character defect of pride and dig in our heels.

The Truth Is: Humility is your strength and your place of power.

The words humility and humble come from the Latin *humilis*, meaning low.

Lao Tsu, author of the *Tao Te Ching*, said:

> "*Why is the sea king of a hundred streams?*
> *Because it lies below them.*
> *This is why the sea is king of a hundred streams.*"

Oceans are the greatest bodies of water because they keep themselves lower than all other waters on the Earth. Being lower, everything flows to the ocean. Thus, an ocean is great because of its humility.

The Latin word can also mean "grounded." Humble, we have two feet firmly planted on the Earth. In a stable, solid place, we can move with purpose and confidence.

Cultivating humility is not easy if you think it means being a doormat or that you must be subject to abuse while meekly suffering in silence. True humility is nothing like that.

We know who we are, and what we want. We know our truth and our power, our position in society, our place in the stream of life, and our reality as a child of the Universe. We are neither better than nor less than. We are protected, cared for, and loved. Nobody can hurt us within our truth.

Humility is vital. It surrenders any ideas we have about removing our shortcomings. Good news. God does for us what we cannot do for ourselves. We make ourselves ready in the first six steps; then we step back and humbly ask, confidently knowing we will be answered.

ACTION ITEMS
Create a treasure map

What do you want? Treasure maps are wonderful ways to create visual representations of your goals and dreams. Working with a group on this fun exercise will help the energy grow. Make one for your twelve-week goal. Make others for any dreams and goals you have.

Create an *I am map*

Who do you want to be? Your I Am Map should represent your desired personality, your spiritual self, and the traits you would like to cultivate. Search for ideas and pictures that vibrate health and wholeness, peace and joy. You will find images that resonate, that ring bells in your mind.

Remember: You are whole and perfect just as you are. The I Am Map does not add anything to you. It awakens that which is already inside.

Do Step 7

Humbly ask God to remove your shortcomings. The process is straightforward but takes practice, patience, and mindfulness. The process is simply:

1. Become Aware
2. Accept
3. Take Action

Trust that situations will arise, opportunities will present themselves to lose the old character defects and practice the new character assets you desire. They will become the new you.

Humility is the key. We do not, we cannot, make these inner changes in ourselves. We can only prepare to receive the gifts our Higher Power has for us.

Reread Week 7 at Least Twice

> *Tithe—Divine Love, flowing through me, blesses and multiplies all that I have, all that I give, and all that I receive. We are blessed to know that Spirit is our Source. God bless! Thank you, God!*

Sing

"I Am So Blessed"
by Karen Drucker

I Am so blessed
I Am so blessed
I Am so grateful, for all that I have
I Am so blessed, I Am so blessed
I Am so grateful, I Am so blessed

We are so blessed
We are so blessed

We are so grateful, for all that we have
We are so blessed, We are so blessed
We are so grateful, We are so blessed

God bless! Thank you, God!

Week 8
Imagination, Intuition, and "Creative Waiting"

> *I invited Intuition to stay in my house when*
> *my roommates went North. I warned her that*
> *I am territorial, and I keep the herb jars in*
> *alphabetical order.*
> *Intuition confessed that she has a "spotty employment*
> *record." She was fired from her last*
> *job for daydreaming.*
> — J. Ruth Gendler, *The Book of Qualities*

Imagination Part II

LAST WEEK, WE talked about the creative power of imagination. You remember that everything that does, can, or ever could exist first had to exist in imagination as an idea.

To really harness the power of imagination, we want to "pull out all the stops," using everything at our disposal: images, words, feelings, touch and smell, excitement and zeal, embellishment—really putting in detail, visualizing our ideas and goals. We want to walk through—in our mind—every step of the process we can conceive of to make our dream come alive.

Using visual aids like vision boards (I Am Maps and treasure maps), you will activate your power of imagination, giving your conscious and subconscious mind physical representations based in physical reality. Seeing images, concepts, words, phrases, and ideas will imprint them on your conscious and subconscious minds!

Using the other spiritual faculties of faith, belief, affirmative prayer, awareness of God's goodness, reliance upon the innate wisdom of the Universe residing in you and more—you will activate your highest good, bringing it into manifestation.

The Truth Is: Your mind and your body cannot feel any difference between something happening in physical reality and something happening in your imagination!

This is easily proven. Close your eyes and try this experiment:

Think of a lemon, yellow, juicy, and tart. Think of how it smells and looks before you cut it. See the knife on the table. Pick it up and cut into the lemon, releasing the fragrance even more strongly.

Do you notice your mouth watering? Perhaps your saliva is already flowing in anticipation of the taste of real, fresh lemon. Or maybe you're scrunching up your face at the thought of its taste?

Now see yourself picking up a half of the lemon. Feel it in your hand. Bring it close to your mouth and bite into the lemon, skin, peel, and fruit.

Did your mouth water even more? Could you see bright yellow? Could you taste lemon in your mind's eye?

Your salivary glands probably responded to your imagination, yet your mind and body acted as if a lemon were in physical reality. It was *only* in your mind. I say *only* because it is grossly underestimating the power of mind and imagination.

Robert Moss, author, mystic, and shamanic teacher of dreams and dreaming, wrote *The Three "Only" Things*. In a short essay about his book, Moss writes:

> The great secret of fulfilling our heart's desires and living in joy and abundance is an open secret. It is a power to be claimed as soon as we awaken to its existence and adopt the tools and habits required to bring it through.
>
> The greater secret is that to work the law of attraction successfully, we need to be aware of which part of us is doing the willing and choosing, and we need to develop a practice that engages the body and the larger self, not merely the calculating ego. We have the tools we need.

> They are at play within us and around us, every day and every night. *They are the three "only" things we too often dismiss as "only" a dream, "only" a coincidence, and "only my imagination." They are incredible guides if we will only give them a little room and respect in our lives.* (Emphasis added)

Far from dismissing these three things with disdain and a wave of our hand ("*Oh, it was only a dream. Oh, it was only a coincidence. Oh, it was only my imagination*"), we must acknowledge these are *real things*, based in *spiritual reality*. If we are wise, we will learn to pay very close attention to these *only* things that the world dismisses as frivolous and inconsequential.

Let's look at what the power of "only my imagination" can achieve in a cosmic way!

In the Old Testament when God says, "Let there be light!" God is activating—with words—an idea first conceived in God's imagination. God calls forth into physical reality that which existed only in God's Imagination.

A better translation, more powerful and direct, is: "Let light be!"

Speaking healing words of truth—Words of Life, according to Myrtle Fillmore—sets up vibrations that the Universe must respond to—calling forth exactly what we expect to see.

Using all our faculties to harness the full power of Imagination, we begin to see the world differently than through ordinary eyes. We see with "eyes of faith."

Picasso said, "Everything you can imagine is real."

He also said, "Painting is a blind man's profession. He paints not what he sees, but what he feels, what he tells himself about what he has seen."

The Truth Is: In physical reality, we do not see the world at all! We see ourselves reflected back!

How We See the World

We think the world is a certain way and accept things without thought or question. "That's just the way things are," we hear people say.

In reality, we never see the world the way it is. The world is a blank screen, a neutral canvas onto which we project our thoughts, beliefs, words, feelings, ideas, and "knowledge." We don't see the world as it is because it is neutral.

The Truth Is: We don't see the world the way it is; *we see the world the way we are!*

Then we project and our projection roars back at us. This happens so instantaneously that we think it's coming *at us* from the outside when it comes forth *from us!*

This is easily proven. Try this experiment:

I have two little dogs, Manny and Erica. Erica is a little teacup Yorkie; Manny is a slightly larger teacup Morkie (Maltese-Yorkie mix). They are cute as can be, right?

I bring them along and ask classes and workshops, "Who thinks Manny and Erica are cute?" Normally, almost everyone's hand goes up.

"Now, who thinks Manny and Erica are scary? Or disgusting? Or not cute?"

Occasionally, someone will buck the conventional wisdom and say, "Well, I just don't like dogs," or "They're not scary, but I don't want them to come near me."

What is the correct answer? Are Manny and Erica cute little furballs, or loathsome creatures who are better off over there, far away?

The Truth Is: The correct answer is *neither.*

They are neither cute nor scary nor disgusting. They are exactly what you say they are.

Here is how it works:

You have your beliefs about dogs: They're cute. They're scary. I don't like little dogs. I don't like big dogs. Then you project your beliefs, thoughts, feelings, ideas, etc. out of your mind, out of your imagination, out onto the blank, neutral world (dogs). Whatever you believe comes roaring back at you. You see what you are looking for, and then you respond as if the dog was [fill in the blank].

So, your inner reality is confirmed by outer reality, but it is nothing more than your inner reality coming back at you.

Out of our minds, out of our imaginations, we create our world—and we get what we look for.

Remember *A Course in Miracles* Lesson 16 from last week: "What gives rise to the perception of a whole world can hardly be called idle."

The Truth Is: You have the power to arrange your world, not by setting it right, but by changing your thoughts and beliefs, so they align with Spiritual Reality. If you don't like what you see—or what you're getting—you can try to rearrange the world around you. Or, you can change your mind.

In other words, you can....

Repent!

Repent simply means "to think again," to change your mind.

In French, "to think" is *penser*. It can also mean "to suppose or to imagine." *Repenser* means "to think again" or "to rethink something." Repent is not an admonition for horrible, irredeemable sinners to fall in line or die, as some would have you believe. Instead, it's a gentle reminder to think a new thought, a better thought. A truer thought. Think "Words of life."

Rethink a thought that doesn't serve you any longer. Does it bring you what you want or what you deserve as a child of the Universe? Is it bringing you your highest and best good? Or is it bringing you misery, despair, lack, and limitation?

The *Tao Te Ching* says that true freedom is freedom from your own thoughts. A person who can question what they think, who can test their thoughts, their assumptions, beliefs, etc., is truly free. They can weigh an old family chestnut against the "evidence of things not seen" and then see what is showing up in their life. Such a person is not hidebound, stuck, and stubborn. They are not clinging to old ways out of pride or ignorance or orneriness. That person is truly free to modify and improve upon their thoughts, and so, upon their lives.

Fortunately, we have all the help we need in this endeavor: The innate wisdom of the Universe, which resides in each and every one of us. We have talked about this already in several different ways (i.e., intuition), but everything points to the same Source of wisdom, the same re-Source, which wants our highest and best good and is ready, willing, and able to show us the way.

Many people seem to have difficulty tuning in to the wisdom and guidance inside them. How does it manifest? How does it communicate? How do we know if, when, and how we are being guided? Is it God or ego? Is it right thinking? Or is it old thinking?

Using intuition doesn't seem easy, yet with a little practice, it can become second nature. In fact, *A Course in Miracles* insists it is natural. Being guided, directed, nurtured, and cared for daily is how we are meant to live as spiritual beings. Even the ability to perform miracles is normal and a more natural way of life. The way we struggle and stumble through life is not only unnatural but unnecessary.

The Holy Spirit is referred to in *A Course in Miracles* as the "voice for God." It does not shout, nor insist, nor bully, nor beg, nor plead. It doesn't communicate in the ways the ego communicates, with its voice of fear, worry, and anger. The voice for God is....

A Still Small Voice

"Go forth and stand upon the mountain.
And, behold, Jehovah passed by,

> *and a great, strong wind*
> *rent the mountains, and broke the rocks;*
> *but Jehovah was not in the wind.*
> *And after the wind, an earthquake; but Jehovah was*
> *not in the earthquake.*
> *And after the earthquake, a fire;*
> *but Jehovah was not in the fire:*
> *and after the fire a still small voice.*
> *And so when Elijah heard it, he wrapped his face in his*
> *mantle, and went out."*
> — Kings 19:11-13

This passage is one of the most beautiful and moving in the Bible. It compares the noise and tumultuous nature of the world and the ego with the peaceful certainty that is of God. The world often thinks that bigger is better, louder is more right. It often believes that might makes right and only the strongest (and cleverest and quickest and sharpest) survives. Our ego thinks it can scheme, manipulate, deceive, take shortcuts, or outwit people or situations, thinking that is the way to success. The ego will cajole, blame, argue, beg, whine, debate, and use sarcasm, wit, logic, anger, hysteria, or any number of other tricks to win the day.

Inner wisdom does none of these things. It is not a demanding, commanding, authoritarian voice of doom and gloom, shame and blame.

The Voice for God is quiet, gentle, loving, soothing, caressing, yet powerful. It is a certain and clear voice that, as *A Course in Miracles* says, "Speaks to me all through the day."

LESSON 49

God's voice speaks to me all through the day.

> It is quite possible to listen to God's voice all day without interrupting your regular activities. The part of your mind in which truth abides is in constant communication with God, whether you are aware of it or not. It is the other part of your mind that functions in the world and obeys the world's laws. It is this

part that is constantly distracted, disorganized, and uncertain.

The part that is listening to the voice for God is calm, always at rest, and wholly certain. It is really the only part there is. The other part is a wild illusion, frantic and distraught, but outside of reality. Try not to listen to it today. Try to identify it with the part of your mind where stillness and peace reign forever. Try to hear God's voice call to you lovingly, reminding you that your Creator has not forgotten you.

The voice for God and intuition are synonymous in my understanding. Call it what you want: Intuition, Conscience, The Holy Spirit, The Voice for God. The "still small voice" is described in some Bible translations as, "The Sound of Sheer Silence."

However you label it, anyone can (with practice) have a clear experience of intuitive "knowing" that is subtle and soft, quiet and gentle, nudging, rather than commanding.

How do we hear this voice? How do we distinguish the voice for God from our random thoughts or the ego's fear-based musings? There lies part of the answer: The voice that speaks fear, lack, and limitation, that is constrained and constricted, can clearly be distinguished from "words of life."

Discerning the voice for God from the ego's voice takes practice and persistence. One of the best things we can do is remember:

Do Not Judge by Appearances

Two stories may help illustrate this in practical, real-world situations:

A Packet of Cookies

A young man was waiting for a flight in an airport. As he had a few hours to wait, he decided to buy a book and a pack of cookies. He went into a quiet area, found a table, sat down, and began reading.

Soon after, a young woman came by and sat down at the table opposite the man. She had a magazine, and started reading, too. The packet of cookies was on the table. The guy opened it and took a cookie. To his surprise, the woman reached over and took one too. This infuriated him, but he didn't say anything.

To his amazement and disbelief, this continued. For each cookie he ate, she ate one, too. It made him fuming mad, but he couldn't react.

Now only one cookie remained. The young woman took the last cookie, divided it in half, and pushed half toward the man.

This was too much! Visibly angry, he snatched up his book, took his things, and stormed off to the gate for boarding.

Taking his seat on the plane, he settled in and went into his bag to find his headphones. Much to his surprise, there in his bag was the *pack of cookies* he bought, untouched.

Realizing his mistake, he felt so ashamed. *He* had been the one in the wrong.

The woman had shared *her* cookies with *him!* She was not at all angry, while he was going mad thinking she was eating his cookies.

By then, of course, it was too late to explain, say thank you, or apologize.

This story is a great example of much of what we encounter in life. We see or hear a situation and we form judgments, opinions, and beliefs based on incomplete information.

Remember: We will never have all the information necessary to judge rightly.

Keep an open mind. Don't judge quickly or harshly. Ask to be shown. The voice for God will respond, showing us what we need to know, revealing the deeper truths in every situation.

Another story I love illustrates how judging by appearances fools us and keeps us from seeing the truth of a situation or a person.

Baby Erik and the Old Man

It was Christmas Day. We were the only family with children in the restaurant. I sat Erik in a highchair. Everyone was quietly eating and talking. Suddenly, Erik squealed with glee, "Hi, there."

He pounded his fat baby hands on the highchair tray, eyes wide with excitement, his mouth in a toothless grin. He wriggled and giggled.

I looked around and saw the source of his merriment. It was a man with a tattered rag of a coat, dirty, greasy, and worn. His pants were baggy, zipper at half-mast, and toes poking out of would-be shoes. His shirt was dirty, and his hair was uncombed and unwashed. His whiskers were too short to be called a beard, and his nose was so varicose it looked like a road map.

We were too far away to smell him, but I was sure he smelled badly. His hands waved and flapped on loose wrists.

"Hi, there, baby; hi there, big boy! I see ya, buster," the man said to Erik.

My husband and I exchanged looks, "What do we do?" Erik continued to laugh and answer, "Hi, hi, there." Everyone in the restaurant noticed and looked at us and then at the man.

The old geezer was creating a nuisance with my beautiful baby. Our meal came. The man began yelling from across the room, "Do ya know patty cake? Do you know peek-a-boo? Hey, look, he knows peek-a-boo."

Nobody thought the old man was cute. He was obviously drunk. My husband and I were embarrassed. We ate in silence—except Erik, who was running through his entire repertoire of cuteness for the admiring skid-row bum, who in turn, reciprocated.

We finally got through the meal and headed for the door. My husband went to pay the check and told me to meet him in the parking lot. The old man sat poised between the door and me. "Lord, just let me out of here before he speaks to me or Erik," I prayed.

As I drew closer to the man, I turned my back, trying to side-step him and avoid any air he might be breathing. As I did, Erik leaned over my arm, reaching with both arms in a baby's "pick-me-up" position. Before I could stop him, Erik propelled himself from my arms to the man's. Suddenly, a very old, smelly man and a very young baby consummated their love relationship.

Erik, in an act of total trust, love, and submission, laid his tiny head upon the man's ragged shoulder. The man's eyes closed, and I saw tears hover beneath his lashes. His aged hands full of grime, pain, and hard labor, gently, so gently, cradled my baby's bottom and stroked his back. No two beings have ever loved so deeply for so short a time.

I stood awestruck. The old man rocked and cradled Erik in his arms for a moment, and then his eyes opened and set squarely on mine. He said in a firm commanding voice, "You take care of this baby."

Somehow, I managed, "I will," from a throat that contained a stone. He pried Erik from his chest, unwillingly, longingly, as though he were in pain. I received my baby, and the man said, "God bless you, ma'am; you've given me my Christmas gift."

I said nothing more than a muttered thanks. With Erik in my arms, I ran for the car. My husband was wondering why I was crying and holding Erik so tightly, and why I was saying, "My God, forgive me."

I had just witnessed Christ's love shown through the innocence of a tiny child who saw no sin, who made no judgment, a child who saw a soul, and a mother who saw a suit of clothes. I was a Christian who was blind, holding a child who was not. I felt it was God asking, "Are you willing to share your son for a moment?" when God shared Jesus for all eternity.

> The ragged old man, unwittingly, had reminded me, "To enter the Kingdom of God, we must become as little children."

These two stories will help us remember: We never have complete information or the complete picture. Functioning from a spiritual place, we must go on faith, trusting there is more going on than meets the eye. We must remember to be guided by the still small voice.

Understanding this doesn't make it easy or comfortable…at first. But, "Practice makes progress," as we grow in experience, confidence, and faith, we will become more accustomed to….

Creative Waiting or Living in the Ambiguity (*Wu Wei*)

Taoists call it *Wu Wei*, or "doing by not doing." Living in the ambiguity is another, deeper form of surrender.

> It is being comfortable *not* knowing.
>
> It is a state of open-minded receptiveness.
>
> It is far away from the certainty of the ego (usually dead wrong) and fully within the certainty of God (always dead on).
>
> It is, "Doing by not-doing."
>
> It is being poised, ready, and receptive.
>
> It is non-doing or non-action.
>
> It is perhaps more accurately described as, "Acting by not-acting."
>
> I call it, "Creative Waiting."

Wu Wei is not about being passive. It is not about allowing people or situations to overwhelm us. It does not mean we let people be abusive.

It is waiting in a state of poised anticipation, actively alert and aware. In other words, we are awake, yet we are still. We are watching for the gate to open, listening for the right time to speak, alert for the right time to strike.

We are in harmony with the "Flow of the Tao," and we intuitively know when and how to move, to take whatever action we might need to take, at the right time and in the right way, with the right attitude of detached and loving care.

This is a deeper commitment to surrender. Learning to be still and listen to intuition — the innate wisdom of the Universe within takes — tremendous practice and patience, but it is the turning point to a new way of life.

In the beginning, we hesitate and are unsure. We want to act, but we think we are being guided, but what if...?

As humans, we are wired to fill in the gaps, make up the unknown parts of the story. We make educated guesses, or we fly blind. How are we ever to get anything right?

The practice of listening to the still small voice gets easier when we do it, when we see it brings us toward our good and away from unnecessary detours and problems.

A story from my life may help illustrate this.

Using Intuition, Part II

In an earlier lesson, I described how I used intuition in my career, in the corridors of New York's state capitol, meeting people to find information to get bills passed. I listened to my inner voice as it guided me to places I hadn't intended to go. I would "synchronistically" meet people I needed to meet and hear things I needed to hear.

This worked, sometimes in a big, dramatic way, in other areas of my life, too. On an early trip to Paris, I didn't know the city well, and my French was not great. I went to a noon recovery meeting, where I briefly met a California man who was on vacation.

Afterward, I went with some others for lunch. I told them I was going to find the Picasso Museum. Someone said it was closed for renovations, but I did not hear that.

Hours later, footsore, thirsty, and tired, I was lost in the winding, medieval streets of the Marais district. I still hadn't found the Picasso Museum. I wanted to sit, but every place was closed or too crowded. I also was having something of an existential crisis. I was traveling alone and had nobody to focus on—to take focus away from my loneliness and other difficult feelings.

(Significantly, the word, "*marais*" means "swamp" in French. And I was in a spiritual and emotional swamp for sure!)

So, lost, tired, lonely, I wondered why I'd come to Paris at all. I felt foolish and generally miserable.

Then, I came to a T in the street. I could go right or left. Right led me out of the Marais, back to the Métro, and out of this physical and emotional morass I was in. Going left took me deeper into the Marais and this seemingly pointless journey.

I paused, focused inward, and asked, "Okay. Which way, God?" The answer I wanted was to go right.

The quiet, but very clear answer I got was "left"—not the answer I wanted.

I sighed, but I listened and turned left. Suddenly, there at a café was the man from California I had met earlier at the meeting. I rushed over like I'd found an oasis in the desert. "Hi!" I said, breathlessly. "I'm so glad to see you! Can I sit for a minute?"

In recovery, if someone needs help, we do what we can, mostly listening and talking. I told him what had happened and what it meant to me to run into him. He was very polite and said some things that were helpful. I really was so self-absorbed that I didn't notice who I was sitting with, other than a person in recovery like me.

Eventually, I calmed down. He asked me where I lived and what I did for work. I told him; then I asked him the same. He said he was an actor from Los Angeles. I asked if he appeared in anything I might have seen.

He mentioned a popular TV drama. Suddenly, it dawned on me. He wasn't just a cast member; he was the star—a big star who had appeared in many feature films as well. I was floored. Up until that moment, I did not recognize him. I felt silly, of course, and happy to meet a movie star...but also something else.

Right then, the dam broke on my existential crisis. Spirit led me in the "wrong" direction. Had I not listened and chose the "logical" answer, I would have missed the connection, and lost the amazing gift God had in store for me.

I used Wu Wei and waited until the right moment to ask Spirit. Then I followed Its "illogical," unmistakably clear guidance toward an answer to my existential crisis.

By plunging headlong into my discomfort, personified by the Marais—swamp—I was led toward a deepening of the frustrating experience I was having in Paris, of being lonely and tired and questioning why I was there. In turn, that counterintuitive guidance and decision led to releasing the tension, frustration, and uneasiness that was building up.

Remember: If you want something to shrink, you must first allow it to expand. In this situation, Spirit knew I needed to lean into the discomfort to break through to a new level of inner resilience and serenity.

A quick second example is striking in its simplicity.

In San Francisco for the first time since I was a child, I went out early one morning to find an open drugstore to grab a few things. After I bought what I needed, I had an inspired thought: cross the street to walk back to the hotel, even though I would have to recross it again. The whisper said, "You'll get a different perspective on the walk back."

So I did. I was barely halfway up the block when I ran into a dear friend and a program sponsor of mine, Jim F, who lived back home in New York, all the way across the country! We laughed and hugged and chatted. What a nice surprise. A "God-incidence."

Neither of us knew the other would be there. I heeded the inspired thought to cross the street, illogical as it seemed, and was richly rewarded by seeing this man who was so important in my spiritual journey.

Using intuition as a guide in every situation never fails. The unchanging, ever-caring voice for God speaks to us all day. And if I am willing to listen and practice getting better at discerning its guiding, loving voice, I will be richly rewarded with invaluable wisdom.

Step 8—Made a list of all persons we have harmed and became willing to make amends to them all.

Step 8 is straightforward:

1. Make a list.
2. Become willing.

Simple, but not easy.

The word "harmed" is key. Whom have we actually harmed?

I define "persons we have harmed," as people whose lives were changed in a negative and significant way because of us. Because of our words and actions, their lives were materially altered in a negative way.

These are not people we offended, or bothered, or ticked off, or people we may have merely disappointed, or other minor mistakes. Our list is *only* people to whom we did or said things with major, life-changing consequences.

We will want to have a sponsor or other trusted advisor work with us and review the list. We don't want to leave anyone out. The people and institutions we have harmed should be on the list, but someone else, too.

Ourselves.

We have harmed ourselves. We need to be on our list. Some feel we should be first on the list. I don't disagree. If it seems right, be number one on your list—but be somewhere on it.

The second part of the step is to become willing to make amends. We must become willing first. For some on our list, it will be easy to make amends, our part is clear.

Yet we may question if others should be on the list at all. Perhaps they harmed us too. Perhaps they harmed us first. Perhaps they harmed us a lot, while maybe we harmed them a little. Why should we make amends to them?

Because we are cleaning up our mess, clearing up our side of the street so we can live healthier and more prosperous lives free from guilt, remorse, shame, and the wreckage of our past.

These amends are for us.

They may help the other person, which is important, but secondary to our primary purpose. Freedom for ourselves is our goal. So, we turn away from what they may have done, and toward what we can change—ourselves and our past—so our future is different, better, brighter, new, and alive with possibilities.

A Course in Miracles states: [Miracles] undo the past in the present and thus release the future. (Chapter 1, paragraph 13). We are actually able, in Spirit, to heal our past so we do not drag it into tomorrow. We release and let it go.

The Sex and Love Addicts Anonymous basic text says, "We closed the ledger on the harms done to us and audited our side of the ledger unsparingly."

Make the list; leave no one out. Let go of old hurts and wrongs. Then you can focus on yourself and clean up what you have done to others. This step pays big dividends as you shall soon see. It promises freedom from shame and guilt as well as freedom from fear.

We have many good things to look forward to as we continue our *Prosperity Now!* process.

ACTION ITEMS

Practice *A Course in Miracles* Lesson 49:
God's Voice speaks to me all through the day.

Listen in deep silence. Be very still and open your mind. Go past [everything] that cover[s] your real thoughts and obscure[s] your eternal link with God.

Sink deep into the peace that waits for you beyond the frantic, riotous thoughts and sights and sounds of this insane world. You do not live here.

We are trying to reach your real home. We are trying to reach the place where you are truly welcome. We are trying to reach God.

Do not forget to repeat today's idea very frequently. Do so with your eyes open when necessary but closed when possible.

And be sure to sit quietly and repeat the idea for today whenever you can, closing your eyes on the world, and realizing that you are inviting God's Voice to speak to you.

Do Step 8

Step eight has two parts.

Make a list and become willing to make amends

Remember the high bar of people we have "harmed." It is likely a short list. Remember that this step is simple. Don't worry or project about what comes after. Keeping our minds in the present moment, the impossibly difficult suddenly becomes possible.

Practice using intuition in everyday situations

Ask, "Which way?" in the grocery store or in a shopping mall. Ask to be shown what to do, whom to call, what to say. Practicing in simple, easy, uncomplicated situations allows us to gain mastery in the use of this spiritual tool. Then, when a serious or difficult situation arises, we will more naturally go within and ask for guidance.

Keep a journal of the miracles that happen

Make notes in your prosperity journal about times you do this and what interesting events occur as a result. What "chance" encounters do you have? What beautiful sights do you see? What miraculous, serendipitous events unfold (always for your greater good)?

Practice *Wu Wei* or "creative waiting"

Learn to be comfortable in the "not knowing" and patiently listen for the Voice for God. It will tell you what you need to know, need to say, need to do.

Our natural, human instinct is often to "Do something! Anything!" to keep from feeling powerless. We feel that if we can exert control, even if that is a futile exercise or a delusion, we at least are "trying." But the fact is that doing "nothing" in the manner of *Wu Wei* is doing something very powerful and very effective. We are marshaling our energies. We are awaiting orders from the High Command. We are preparing ourselves to follow instructions. We are alert and awake. We will act, if at all, when the moment is right, when the time is ripe for our part in the drama. An actor who comes in off-cue ruins the play. We may not know our lines, but we are confident we will be told what to say, what to do, and when to do it.

Creative waiting is extremely difficult for most of us at first. We don't yet have the experience of things working out better than we could possibly imagine. But, as suggested above about using intuition in everyday situations, practicing in easy, uncomplicated situations will give us a measure of mastery, so when a difficult or serious situation arises, we will be better able to use this powerful tool. Try it!

Reread Week 8 At Least Twice

Tithe—*Divine Love, flowing through me, blesses and multiplies all that I have, all that I give and all that I receive. We are blessed to know that Spirit is our Source. God bless! Thank you, God!*

Sing

"I Am So Blessed"
by Karen Drucker

I Am so blessed
I Am so blessed
I Am so grateful, for all that I have
I Am so blessed, I Am so blessed
I Am so grateful, I Am so blessed

We are so blessed
We are so blessed
We are so grateful, for all that we have
We are so blessed, We are so blessed
We are so grateful, We are so blessed

God bless! Thank you, God!

Week 9

Defenselessness Is Safety

Life begins at the end of your comfort zone.
— Neale Donald Walsch

Even More About Surrender

WE'VE SAID A lot about surrender over eight weeks. Surrender is in every step. It is the antidote to our twin problems of powerlessness—over people and circumstances—and unmanageability in our thinking and our life.

Looking at areas of our lives, we see they might not be what we'd like them to be. Maybe they are less than we hoped for: our finances, with high debts and low funds, or maybe health is a concern, or relationships, or addiction, or constant busyness, constant worry, obsessive thinking, or general depression, confusion, sadness, whatever.

Maybe we have big ideas, but they don't pan out. Maybe we try to "make things happen," rather than surrendering and allowing God to take over, and we fall short. Admitting that a Higher Power can relieve our human powerlessness is vital to finding real, lasting solutions to our life issues, financial woes, and other dilemmas.

Only by admitting that we have a problem will we see a need for a solution. Until we surrender—let go and let God—we won't have a desire to do what's needed to turn the ship in a new, positive, and productive direction.

We surrender our old beliefs and ideas to put "new wine into new wineskins"—new ideas into a new consciousness.

So far, through eight weeks, maybe you've noticed the glimmer of a deeper level of surrender, beyond merely releasing old, outdated ideas.

Last week we spoke of *Wu Wei* or acting through non-action. Doing without doing. Instead of forcing things, the Taoist uses the Tao—the force that underpins the entire Universe. Flowing and harmonizing with this force, life goes more smoothly. Things seem to work out, often not in ways we could predict. Allowing and waiting, we act naturally and spontaneously when the time is right.

Wu Wei requires a profound willingness to question your ego's need to be right. It can be earthshaking to your entire belief system. You must awaken to the thought that maybe you really don't know anything at all.

Remember: We go through life with incomplete information. While it is normal and necessary to gather data and facts, and to hear people's opinions and experiences before deciding, eventually, we have to decide, or we are doomed to remain paralyzed "deciding not to decide."

So, What to Do?

Our way out of this dilemma: Deepen your reliance on your intuition—the still small voice—the voice for God. That inherit wisdom of the Universe that resides in you knows more and sees farther ahead than you ever will.

To get comfortable relying on this voice, you must surrender your typical (normal) human inclination to figure things out.

Surrender means acknowledging that you might not be the best judge of circumstances. Admitting you are not the smartest, are not omniscient, and are frequently wrong is daunting—and freeing!

Be aware that this realization can set up a defensive reaction. Paradoxically, the ego might become even more insistent on having its own way, and will often double down in its wrongness. Pigheaded and obstinate, it will insist on having its way, even in the face of overwhelming evidence to the contrary, wholly from fear.

Letting go of the illusion of control is scary.

But, as we have learned about Spirit, the truth is 180 degrees away from what the world believes. We believe we are safe when we plan, figure, manipulate, and defend our position when questioned or "attacked."

A Course in Miracles points out that we are safest—perfectly safe—when we don't defend or attack, explain or debate with others.

In My Defenselessness, My Safety Lies

Lesson 153 in the *A Course in Miracles Workbook* is one of the hardest to understand, much less practice. But understanding it gives us a prescription for safety in all circumstances. The appearance that the world is unsafe gives rise to fear, and a need to control, to defend ourselves and our ideas.

The Lesson says, in part: "The world gives rise but to defensiveness. For threat brings anger, anger makes attack seem reasonable, honestly provoked, and righteous in the name of self-defense."

The Truth Is: We are defending the small scraps we have accumulated against imaginary enemies and against an illusion of lack and limitation.

This defensiveness sets us up for a double whammy. The fear-based ego believes we are in danger, and it tells us we need to defend ourselves. This belief that we need to be defensive, because we fear lack, we fear attack, we fear loss, loneliness, and unworthiness—it tells us two things:

- We are weak, and
- We must set up defenses…

…which we do, while knowing in our heart that these defenses will not work.

The lesson paints a dark picture of this dynamic. Most of us are not even aware of how important and how seriously dysfunctional it is. It states:

> Defenses are the costliest of all the prices which the ego would exact. In them lies madness in a form so grim that hope of sanity seems but to be an idle dream, beyond the possible. The sense of threat the world encourages is so much deeper, and so far beyond the frenzy and intensity of which you can conceive, that

you have no idea of all the devastation it has wrought. You are its slave. *You know not what you do, in fear of it.* You do not understand how much you have been made to sacrifice, who feel its iron grip upon your heart. You do not realize what you have done to sabotage the holy peace of God by your defensiveness. (Emphasis added.)

We now appear doubly doomed, and ultimately, completely lost and confused. It seems we have no way out of this dilemma.

Our ego sets us up, we act out of fear, and we lose every time—lose sight of the precious gifts of Spirit that are rightfully ours: love, sanity, serenity, joy, happiness, peace, abundance, courage, and finally, life itself.

"In my defenselessness, my safety lies" is the ultimate surrender. We are called upon to halt, put down our weapons, shields and armor, and await further instructions. Now defenseless, we have no choice but to rely upon the voice of God—the innate wisdom of the Universe residing in us—to handle every situation and answer every question.

Surrender to win is paradoxical in the world's eyes, but it works.

Relying on our own resources, we will always be on guard, never secure. Relying on the Universe, turning our will and life over to the *care* of God (Step 3), we flow with the Way (Tao) of how things really work—of how things really are—rather than against it.

When we forget our Source, we feel weak, and believe we are weak. That illusion causes us to compensate. We desperately set up defenses to "protect" ourselves.

The pull against surrender is powerful. "Stay strong" is constantly reinforced in messages from parents, friends, family, television, social media, the news, religion, etc.

Tuning in to the Source inside of us and listening, we gain better understanding. As we grow in confidence, we act on our intuition. This becomes our true source of information, power, assurance, and confidence—a source the world could never provide.

True Freedom

As we noted, the *Tao Te Ching* says, "True freedom is freedom from your own ideas." Question everything you think. Ask, "Is it true?" This is a powerful way to be free. Without questioning, we have no choice but to believe what we think.

In questioning our assumptions, beliefs, and thoughts, we are free to choose, keeping what works, throwing away what doesn't, and freeing ourselves to choose again.

James Allen's groundbreaking book, *As a Man Thinketh*, takes its title from the Bible, Proverbs 23:7, "As a man thinketh in his heart, so he is."

Allen writes, "The Vision that you glorify in your mind, the Ideal that you enthrone in your heart—this you will build your life by, this you will become."

The Truth Is: You are the creator of your reality and of your life. Hold a vision of the life you would love to have, and you will live into that vision!

And, the life you see now is a result of the vision you have been holding, good or not so good, consciously or unconsciously. We are striving to live consciously awake and purposefully alive.

Understanding, embodying, and integrating these ideas leads to abundance. We have begun a holistic, psychic change that comes about when we repent (rethink) and deeply and profoundly change our thinking.

As we think, so we are—and so our life is. Remember, we are highly creative beings made in the same mold as the Creative Source of everything.

The Truth Is: We are highly attractive beings.

We attract exactly what we are looking for, consciously or unconsciously. Our vibration—thinking, feeling, believing, knowing, desiring, hoping, saying, doing—sets up a vibration, and the Universe responds perfectly.

A Consciousness of Lack vs. a Consciousness of Abundance

Seek ye first the Kingdom of Heaven....

The power of our thinking creates our life and the world we see. We have emphasized this in various ways throughout *Prosperity Now!*

We can think about changing our thinking, but that doesn't work. To really change our thinking, our life, our experiences, and our world, we must take action. We must, "Begin it now!"

The Truth Is: We cannot think ourselves into new ways of action. We must act ourselves into new ways of thinking.

Suppose you want to learn to swim. What would you do? Thinking about swimming, reading books about swimming, talking to people about swimming, watching other people swim, and studying theories about buoyancy and the physics of swimming are not bad, but they will not make you a swimmer.

Even getting into a bathing suit and getting in the water will not make you a swimmer. Wade around all you want, splash water, dunk down and get your whole head wet. Still not a swimmer. The only way to learn how to swim is to jump in! Allow the water to take over your body, and float, sink, or swim.

Jump in! It is the very definition of "A leap of faith."

The imperative that we must take action is doubly true for building a life wholly reliant on Spirit.

"Faith without works is dead" (James 2:20) means action is required to live by spiritual laws that will bring you your greatest good. Tithing is a powerful action that demonstrates faith.

Tithing effectively demonstrates *to yourself* that you are invested in your spiritual journey. You are taking your feet off the bottom of the ocean and trusting in its buoyancy and your innate wisdom to keep you afloat, financially and in all ways.

Tithing demonstrates that you are "seeking first the Kingdom." You could do all the activities in this course and you would make progress. Yet, if you want to really move your consciousness into higher orbit and deeper levels of awareness, nothing beats the action of tithing for dramatic results.

Faith? Yes! But action is crucial.

Now when we act, it is no longer based on blind faith, but on our lived experience that can be built upon, replicated, and expanded with stronger faith to fit new challenges and meet new goals.

Belief activates faith and must be followed by action. A couple of Bible stories illustrate this—one involves someone who acts and the other is about someone who doesn't.

The Widow's Mite

> *"Jesus sat down opposite the treasury and observed the crowd putting money into the treasury. Many rich people put in large sums. A poor widow also came and put in two small coins worth a few cents.*
> *"Calling his disciples, he said to them, 'Amen, I say to you, this poor widow put in more than all the others. For they contributed from their surplus wealth, but she, from her poverty, has contributed all she had, her whole livelihood.'"*
> — Mark 12:41-44

The story of the Widow's Mite in the Gospel of Mark is a powerful story of lack consciousness versus a consciousness of abundance and of taking action.

Donations to the temple treasury in Jerusalem supported the temple's work. The funds also supported widows and orphans, the sick, crippled, and elderly. Their lot was not good. The alms they received from the temple were not much, but they helped keep people from starving.

The wealthy came to pay their temple tax. Many made a show of their giving, so that others would see how pious and generous they were. Jesus calls his disciples to watch what happens. A widow comes to the temple and puts in two small coins, two "mites."

First, she was not expected to give anything because she would normally *receive* charity from the treasury. Yet she gives anyway.

Jesus rightly notes that she gives "more than all the others" because she gives all she has—100 percent of her wealth, while the rich, showy folk give just a small portion of their total belongings.

Jesus then goes further and says something paradoxical: "She gave out of her poverty (or lack)," while the rich gave out of their surplus. In other words, they gave from funds they didn't need, while she gave from funds she needed. She gave "from her poverty."

So.... Who had more faith? She did!

Who gave more? She did!

Who has a consciousness of abundance? She does!

Giving as she did, from her lack, does not mean she lacked consciousness. She gives in complete faith that she will be taken care of; she will be rewarded for her action—hers is faith in action.

The wealthier members of the temple do not have this faith; they do not demonstrate their trust and belief in abundance. They have a consciousness of lack, giving from their surplus. She has a consciousness of abundance, giving out of her poverty.

This consciousness dichotomy is expressed in our next parable.

The Rich Young Man

I alluded to this story in an earlier week. A "rich young man" approaches Jesus and asks what he must do to enter the Kingdom of Heaven. Jesus tells him the things he must do. The man replies that he does all those things.

> *"Jesus said, 'One thing you lack: Go, sell everything you have and give to the poor, and you will have treasure in heaven. Then come, follow me.'*
>
> *"At this the man's face fell. He went away sad because he had great wealth. And Jesus said, 'How difficult it is for the rich to enter the Kingdom of God!'"*
>
> — Mark 10:21-23

Here, Jesus seems to be saying that it is hard for rich people to enter heaven (that state of perfect peace and love) because they are rich, but that is not the case. Again, what *seems* to be true is 180 degrees away from the truth in Spirit.

I think the meaning here is that he cannot enter Heaven because he is attached to his possessions. He fears their loss. It seems he does not trust that he will be taken care of, putting trust in wealth, rather than God.

Putting earthly things before Spirit, we will never be truly secure. We are "defending" against loss, "storing up riches" where they can be stolen. Spirit is our solid foundation for abundance.

Then, right after, Jesus doubles down. He says, "It is easier for a camel to pass through the eye of the needle than it is for a rich man to enter the Kingdom of Heaven."

Some say "The Eye of the Needle" was a narrow gate into the city of Jerusalem. A person riding a camel could not pass through the gate with their heavily laden saddle bags slung across the camel's back. They would have to dismount, remove their possessions from the camel's back, and lead the camel through the "Eye of the Needle."

You couldn't enter Jerusalem (whose name means the City of Peace) *and* cling to your possessions.

One can be wealthy *and* have the Kingdom of Heaven, but one has to choose; one has to come first—and we know which one that is.

> *"Seek first the Kingdom of Heaven, and all things will be added unto you."*
> — Matthew 6:33

This is not a platitude, but a formula for the law in action. We put God first when we offer our tithes first. When we seek spiritual solutions to our dilemmas, then all other things—for our highest and best good—will be ours.

The Universe Responds to Our Consciousness

Another difficult Bible verse relates to this "upside-down" belief in defense as safety:

> *"For them who have, more will be given. But for those who have not, even that little will be taken away."*
> — Matthew 13:12

Wait! What? If I have a lot, I'll get more? But if I'm poor, and have little, even that little will be taken from me? What kind of spiritual justice is that?

Again, what *appears* true is 180 degrees away from reality, from truth in Spirit. The verse is saying: If I have a consciousness of abundance with many positive ideas and beliefs; if I have lots going on, good, wholesome, productive, healthy, worthwhile, enriching, enlivening, loving things; if I have an abundance of ideas, projects, plans, goals, etc., then I am living and embodying a prosperity consciousness.

And so, my life will be full. I know I have enough. I have more than enough.

This is my tithing affirmation:

I have enough!
I have more than enough!
I have more than enough to share!
And, I am ready to receive more!

I keep the flow flowing, keep the channel open. I know a deep and wide consciousness of abundance is like a free-flowing and nourishing river. Tithing lets me keep God first, sharing from my poverty (not from my surplus). Tithing generates feelings of security and safety. I know I will be protected and cared for.

You've heard that if you want something done, give it to a busy person. This is that axiom in action!

One who is overflowing with abundance, generosity, Words of Life, and a new consciousness is in the flow of life and is ready to enter the Kingdom of Heaven.

But if my ideas are few, if my words are small, my thinking impoverished, full of fear and lack—in effect I am saying to the Universe, "I am not worthy. I am poor in body, mind, and Spirit, unworthy and undeserving." And even the little that I have, I will lose.

The rich, young man puts riches first and walks away sad because his consciousness is in scarcity, not in abundance.

The Universe is not punishing, tricking, hurting, or playing games. It is quite responsive to our vibrations, our deepest thinking and feelings. It always says "Yes!"

If we say we can't, we won't, we are afraid, we will fail, things are against us, then the Universe says, "Yes! You are right!" And we get exactly what we look for and expect in our heart of hearts.

If we say,

"*I have enough.*
I have more than enough.
I have more than enough to share.
And I am ready to receive more!"

...then the Universe says, "Yes! You are, and here you go."

Be like the widow. Give in faith from your poverty, and "all things will be added unto you," first in Spirit and in mind and then in your physical reality.

Worthiness

One vital factor that must be mentioned at this point is the idea of "worthiness." At some level, many of us have a deep-seated belief that we are unworthy. This idea is summed up perfectly in Marianne Williamson's well-known quote:

> Our deepest fear is not that we are inadequate. Our deepest fear is that we are powerful beyond measure. It is our light, not our darkness that most frightens us. We ask ourselves, "Who am I to be brilliant, gorgeous, talented, fabulous?" Actually, who are you not to be? You are a child of God. Your playing small does not serve the world.
>
> There is nothing enlightened about shrinking so that other people won't feel insecure around you. We are all meant to shine, as children do. We were born to make manifest the glory of God that is within us. It's not just in some of us; it's in everyone. And as we let our own light shine, we unconsciously give other people permission to do the same. As we are liberated from our own fear, our presence automatically liberates others.

Hearing those words, how do you feel? It's about *you*!

Say it in the first person to yourself. "My deepest fear is not that I am inadequate. My deepest fear is that *I am* powerful beyond measure."

All of the ideas in *Prosperity Now!* are practical and useable. They are effective and powerful. They work!

Reflect back to our earliest lesson on conflicted thinking—if I pray for *this* but believe the opposite, my prayer is not going to manifest what I say, but what I *expect*.

Knowing that you *are* worthy is vital to a successful, prosperous life, to shining your light, and giving other people permission to do the same.

God does not make junk! You have no missing parts. You are whole and complete and worthy of all the good God has in store for you. Step up and claim it. It is your rightful inheritance.

You deserve it. You are worthy.

Step 9—Made direct amends to such people, wherever possible, except when to do so would injure them or others.

This step can bring up a lot of fear, but the reason to do it is simple: to free ourselves from our past.

It is an exercise in extreme self-care. Do not fear and do not delay.

Done with the understanding that we must not injure others in the process, this step will free us and the people to whom we make our amends. This is a wonderful thing. We want to be free from past mistakes, so we can go forward into the future without the weight and stumbling blocks of yesterday holding us back.

A Course in Miracles has a lot to say about this process. It says:

> Miracles...undo the past in the present, and thus release the future.
>
> Miracles are natural signs of forgiveness. Through miracles you accept God's forgiveness by extending it to others.
>
> Miracles restore the mind to fullness. By atoning for lack, they establish perfect protection.
>
> (Text, Ch. 1. paragraphs 13, 21, 34)

When we make amends for wrongs we have done, we free our minds, bodies, and spirits from the old ghosts we have been carrying of old events that color our vision, block our growth, and cause feelings of shame and guilt, fear, anger, and self-pity.

We must do no harm while taking Step 9. We cannot free ourselves at another's expense. It is best to do this with the aid of a spiritual advisor who is well-versed in the twelve steps.

The Truth Is: We cannot buy our peace of mind at another's expense!

For example, if we had an affair, and our spouse knows nothing of it, we could harm them by revealing it.

If we have stolen money from someone, revealing that may put us in legal jeopardy.

Again, weigh the consequences with help from another who has experience. Will we harm others, including ourselves if we lose our job or go to jail? What if we have children at home depending on us?

Amends repair damage we have caused. We want to set things right, not cause more damage.

Plenty of good literature exists from many twelve-step fellowships on Step 9. You may want to read some of it before embarking on your amends.

Some people, full of zeal and enthusiasm, want to rush right out and make amends to everyone immediately. Understandable but misguided. Caution is a good watchword, but don't procrastinate either.

Getting this step done will pay big dividends for our self-esteem, our prosperity, and our future!

Step 9 Denial and Affirmation

I move forward by letting go of the past.
I am at peace with my past.
I am grateful and happy to experience new joy!

Do Not Be Fooled by Fear

Ancient maps outlined the "Known World" of that time. The edges of the map marked the limits of their knowledge. The unknown areas were labeled: "Here there be monsters."

When we contemplate making changes, we are afraid of what might be in store for us. The human mind often projects horror movies, rather than positive and successful outcomes.

What will life be like after? What will happen if I leave a job to follow my passion? Will it work financially? If I go back to school at my age, what lies at the end of that path?

Do not fear. There are no monsters lurking, only limitless possibilities!

Recognize the voice that speaks fear (the ego). Tune it out. Tune into the voice that speaks peace, encouragement, prosperity, and love.

Jon Mundy, my friend and *Course in Miracles* teacher, says our minds are radio receivers. They pick up the signals we tune in to, often radio station WEGO, the voice of fear and lack. It's loud and it plays all the hits.

But we can change the dial to station WGOD to hear a still small voice speaking peace. It is quieter, but in tune with reality. We choose which one we listen to each moment of the day.

My friend, Robert Moss, prolific author of books on dreams and dreaming and a shamanic teacher, emphasizes how to live life by the symbols, signs, and messages we receive at the various levels of dreaming (including on the plane of waking reality). He says, "That which you are seeking is seeking you."

In dreaming reality, a monster may appear—a big scary bear, a dragon, or another frightening image. Our natural reaction is to flee. Using his "dream re-entry" techniques, we can turn to face the fear and confront the demon.

A good pronoic himself, Robert demonstrates that the monster is really a valuable guide or teacher. It may bear a gift for us. The Universe is good. Nothing is out to harm us. All things are here to help us along the way.

The bear gives us a healing hug. The witch offers valuable information. The lion turns out to be a protector. Even dying in a dream can be a signal: time to lose our old life, to have a new and better life.

The Truth Is: We are always safe and protected. We have nothing to fear. Step up and step out in faith. Know you have many good things to look forward to.

ACTION ITEMS
Review Your Surrender on a Deeper Level

Each spiritual principle and each step means surrendering old thinking. As you make notes of your review in your prosperity journal, you will find areas that come easy to you, that are fun. You will also find others that are difficult, where you have resistance or outright rebellion. "I'm not doing that!"

Pay attention to the difficult areas. A sincere effort in those areas often brings the biggest payoff. If you are having trouble letting go, be patient with yourself. This is a marathon, not a sprint—it is a lifetime process. Relax and trust that the Universe is supporting your every effort.

Practice and Meditate on *A Course in Miracles* Lesson 153

In Defenselessness My Safety Lies

Defenselessness is strength. It testifies to recognition of the Christ in you…choice is always made between Christ's strength and your own weakness, seen apart from Him. Defenselessness can never be attacked, because it recognizes strength so great attack is folly, or a silly game a tired child might play, when he becomes too sleepy to remember what he wants.

Defensiveness is weakness. It proclaims you have denied the Christ and come to fear …. What can save you now from your delusion of an angry god, whose fearful image you believe you see at work in all the evils of the world? What but illusions could defend you now when it is but illusions that you fight?

We will not play such childish games today. For our true purpose is to save the world, and we would not exchange for foolishness the endless joy our function offers us. We would not let our happiness slip by because a fragment of a senseless dream happened to cross our minds, and we mistook the figures in it for the Son of God, its tiny instant for eternity.

We look past dreams today and recognize that we need no defense because we are created unassailable, without all thought or wish or dream in which attack has any meaning. Now we cannot fear, for we have left all fearful thoughts behind. And in defenselessness we stand secure, serenely certain of our safety now, sure of salvation; sure, we will fulfill our chosen purpose, as our ministry extends its holy blessing through the world.

Do Step 9

Use your twelve-step sponsor or a spiritual advisor to work on this important step. It is vital we do it correctly so we do not harm the people we make amends to or others. You do not have to do this alone, and indeed, you should find someone with experience to guide you.

Use Your Step 9 Affirmation

> *I move forward by letting go of the past.*
> *I am at peace with my past.*
> *I am grateful and happy to experience new joy!*

Review Your Goal for The Course

The goal you set in Week 1 should be checked consistently. See if you are on track toward it. Keep careful notes in your prosperity journal about what you are doing to consistently move in that direction.

Reread Week 9 at Least Twice

Use This New Tithing Affirmation

> *I have enough!*
> *I have more than enough!*
> *I have more than enough to share!*
> *And, I am ready to receive more!*

> ***Tithe**—Divine Love, flowing through me, blesses and multiplies all that I have, all that I give and all that I receive. We are blessed to know that Spirit is our Source. God bless! Thank you, God!*

Sing

"I Am So Blessed"
by Karen Drucker

I Am so blessed
I Am so blessed
I Am so grateful, for all that I have
I Am so blessed, I Am so blessed
I Am so grateful, I Am so blessed

We are so blessed
We are so blessed
We are so grateful, for all that we have
We are so blessed, We are so blessed
We are so grateful, We are so blessed

God bless! Thank you, God!

Week 10

Beyond the Limits of Your Sight

> *Piglet noticed that even though he had
> a Very Small Heart,
> it could hold a rather large amount of
> Gratitude.*
>
> — A. A. Milne

Love, Love, Love

A WORD WE HAVEN'T used too much so far in this course, but one infused in everything we are discussing, is love.

Love is often misunderstood, given multiple meanings, misused, and mistaken for a myriad of other things that may or may not have anything to do with actual love.

If we say, "God is Love," and understand that "God is Everything," then we can easily see that "Everything is love" in some form or another.

Someone wise once said, "Everything is either an expression of love, or else it is a cry for love." That pretty much sums up every possibility under the sun!

It is easy for most of us to see God/Love in a beautiful sunset, a baby, a tree, or other manifestations of nature. We can see love in a compassionate friend, a generous and kind stranger, a thoughtful gesture, or a loving embrace. But what about when something is troubling, difficult, confusing, or downright tragic? As we said in earlier lessons, to find gratitude in the midst of a tragedy—finding good in a sad situation, finding love in the midst of chaos or negativity—is very hard.

The Truth Is: We often focus on what is breaking down and going away. And we fail to notice the new, good thing trying to break through.

Remember Isaiah? "Behold! I am doing something new. Can you not see it?" God is always manifesting our good because God loves us unconditionally. God cannot help but to love us. Not because God is a being who is loving, but because God is Love Itself! And we are an expression of that love.

Seeing God's Love in our finances gets us out of the mindset that money is somehow separate, different—or evil, as some think of it. Or maybe just distasteful and unworthy of serious consideration, spiritually.

Nonsense! Your labor, your livelihood, the physical and financial support for your life, your comfort, your needs, your family, and your wellbeing are directly tied to God's love. Seeing love in everything means seeing God in these matters as well.

Does this mean those with more money are loved more by God? Again, nonsense!

Remember: We use tithing to open our consciousness to the fruits of the Spirit, to things that no amount of money could ever buy: peace of mind, hope, joy, contentment, generosity, honesty, compassion, etc.

By including finances in our spiritual toolkit, we are engaging a powerful "worldly" concept and infusing it with spiritual meaning and purpose. Our prayer in action, our affirmations and denials made manifest in physical reality, our gratitude as a vehicle to go beyond mere feeling, and our love, tangible in many ways (how we speak, touch, how we see another, how we help, support, encourage, teach, embrace, smile) now have another facet to them: How we receive and how we give.

The Truth Is: To give and to receive are one in truth—from *A Course in Miracles* Lesson 108 is a physical, tangible demonstration of the oneness of all life.

If we give, we receive that which we give and more. If we receive, we are blessed, and we bless the giver with our receptivity and our gratitude.

This idea demonstrates the oneness of all: God, Love, You, Me… everything:

> Here are both giving and receiving seen as different aspects of one *thought* whose truth does not depend on which is seen as first, nor which appears to be in second place. Here it is understood that both occur together, that the *thought* remain complete. And in this understanding is the base on which all opposites are reconciled because they are perceived from the same frame of reference which unifies this *thought*.

Give in love. Receive in love. Recognize the oneness inherent in all transactions, in all exchanges. Recognize the love that is in constant circulation, like the water cycle, replenishing and increasing all life.

Attitude of Gratitude

It is a growing belief among many that an "attitude of gratitude" enfolds a person with a vital, healing energy. A grateful person is immersed in wellness and peace of mind, allowing them to weather all troubles and meet all challenges.

In a state of gratitude, we see things clearly, judging not by appearances but with right judgment. We see the truth of things because we are deeply in touch with the all-goodness of Universal Mind.

Feelings of gratitude are more powerfully expressed by action. Gratitude can be expressed by thankfulness, appreciation, contentment, joy, relief, or other qualities acknowledging our good fortune.

While feeling grateful helps us have a positive, glass-half-full perspective, it only goes so far. Gratitude without action is dead, perhaps. As an action verb—love in action, appreciation in action, joy in action—gratitude expands and increases!

Moving from an inner feeling to an outward energy reaches out to touch others, affecting people, changing the world and ourselves. In prosperity terms, "What we appreciate, appreciates!"

Money in an interest-bearing account appreciates and grows larger. When we gratefully put all our spiritual wealth, ideas, beliefs, faith, successes, failures, indeed, the sum of all of our experiences, in our spiritual bank account (higher consciousness) we take an interest and our spiritual wealth grows.

As Reverend Crystal Muldrow, former minister at Unity Church in Albany, likes to point out, when we are "grateful," we experience the Great-Fullness of Life, in all of its many wonderful, powerful, and exciting aspects. A heart that has a "Great-Fullness" has expanded, indeed, and is able to hold much richness.

The power of gratitude shapes our perceptions, our lives, and our world. It is so powerful that it works "in all of our affairs"—the pleasurable and welcome aspects of life, and the difficult and more troublesome aspects as well.

When we receive something we like, something nice or fun or what we would call good, it is easy to appreciate it, feel gratitude, and take action to reflect our gratitude. But when something unpleasant happens—sudden job loss, divorce, illness, trouble with a loved one, or worst of all, the death of someone we love—what then?

In Week 6, we talked about gratitude in the midst of a storm. Looking past what we are losing, we can eventually begin to see the good coming through. It's not easy, and yes, it takes time. But the good is always there….

How do we find gratitude in the face of disappointments, tragedies, and broken dreams? How can anyone suggest there's something to be grateful for in a terrible situation? This is where an attitude of gratitude really shows its power and capacity to change our minds, our lives, and our world.

> *"Some of your greatest advances you have judged as failures, and some of your deepest retreats you have evaluated as success."*
> — *A Course in Miracles*, Text-18.V.1.6

Often, we cannot judge rightly. Remember *Tao Te Ching*, Poem 20 that asked, "What is the difference between success and failure?" What is an advancement, and what is a setback? What is a triumph? What is tragedy?

Of course, any significant loss is sad. These events cause difficult feelings, from rage and anger to sadness and depression. Yet with time, patience, and a willingness to see beyond appearances, we can find gratitude…for the time we had with someone, what they taught us, the wisdom they shared, the joys and the sorrows we shared.

As I mentioned in Week 4, poet Laurie Anderson remarked upon the death of her husband, musician and poet, Lou Reed, "The purpose of death is to release love." Think about that. The death of someone close to us is an experience of tremendous grief. And is that grief a self-centered feeling because we lost someone? Or is it an upwelling of pent-up love that was lying dormant—in potential—until death opened the floodgates, triggering an outpouring of grief/love?

This powerful awareness is summed up in oft-heard expressions: "Don't wait until I'm dead to send me flowers. I don't want to hear at my funeral how much you miss me. Call me now."

Joni Mitchell expressed this in her song "Big Yellow Taxi" when she reminded us we do not know what we have until it's gone—and that if we pave over nature, we will miss when it's gone, which is too late.

Of course, we also need gratitude for the good things. Some people receive tremendous blessings and toss them away. Some people receive their good like a greedy child, saying, "Thanks. What else?"

Share your gratitude for the good, amazing, unexpected blessings, the hard-won successes, joys, and prizes. Appreciate your good and it will appreciate.

But in solemn and difficult times, the tragedies and the setbacks, take time in your grief to see the "Blessin' in the lesson," the silver lining in the dark cloud. There are gifts there, too. They make the difficult easier and the painful less painful. They soften the edges of our anger and quiet our confusion. Looking back in gratitude, we can see more clearly the path that brought us to where we are today. We can more easily accept things the way they are.

All Things Work Together

I have been through a number of difficulties, and I can honestly say the pain and sadness fade after the intensity has passed. The twelve-step process discharges negative energies, healing the past once and for all. I can attest that my present-day serenity comes from knowing the truth of Romans 8:28, "All things work together for good for those who love God."

This principle is as true as anything I can offer you. In the flow—judging rightly, surrendering, allowing, trusting with faith—everything furthers our good, even if it appears difficult or unwelcome, not according to our plan or our expectations of what is supposed to happen.

"All things" means not just some things or the things we like. Looking back with the softening of time and the right perspective, seen through the eyes of gratitude, events take on new meaning. There was a reason, a *good* reason, a purpose to what happened. It was not in vain, but a necessary occurrence to help us along our path.

The Peace That Passes All Understanding

"And the peace of God, which passeth all understanding, shall keep your hearts and minds" (Philippians 4:7). This is a promise I know to be true. That kind of peace money cannot buy. It is available any time we choose. A quick story from my life illustrates this.

In the fall of 1996, soon after I was diagnosed with HIV, I connected with a fellow person in recovery who took me to a spiritual retreat for people with the virus. There I met a lot of other People with AIDS (PWAs), all of whom had been diagnosed before me. Many had large pillboxes to carry medications and vitamins.

Many also had worried looks on their faces and spoke in fearful tones about the medications and how "toxic" they were, and how bad some of the side effects were. I got a lot of fear-based advice that gave me a lot of anxiety.

Right after the retreat, I went with friends to a recovery convention on Cape Cod. The driver was a dear friend who had been HIV-positive for many years. In the backseat, I was yammering on and on about my situation: "I need to start medications; my condition is bad; I don't want to take them; everything I've heard is bad news. Yadda. Yadda. Yadda."

This dilemma had me in a real bind, and my blathering got on my friend's nerves. Finally, he'd had enough. "Oh, just shut up, Mary!" he said. "Get off the cross; somebody else needs the wood!" (Gay men have fluid pronouns and a great way of expressing themselves, don't you think?)

Then he said: "I'm taking Epivir, Zerit, and Crixivan, and it's working great."

That was it! I tell you all my fear ceased. All my worry disappeared in literally a split second. God spoke (in a very campy way) and I had my answer.

I literally lost all fear. I *knew* I would be all right. I was certain that the new drug "cocktail" would work for me.

I experienced "the peace that passes all understanding" because there was no worldly explanation for the shift in my consciousness. Nothing, absolutely nothing, had changed on the outside. I had changed. My old consciousness gave way to a fresh, new (and true) belief, one that did not come from "John-mind" but from the Universe.

Soon after, I began that regimen, and used gratitude to bless the pills. I said, "Thank you, God. I can afford these medications. I affirm that they will work 1,000 times better than normal and with no side-effects whatsoever. And so it is, and so it must be!"

I declared that they were not toxic, but life-affirming, and they worked perfectly. Within a few months, the HIV was suppressed and my immune system began to be restored. Thank You, God!

Don't Ask Why!

Along with finding good and gratitude in every situation and taking action, it is not particularly helpful to ask "why" a thing happened (or didn't happen). Here is why:

If I am *not* spiritually fit, no answer will satisfy me.

If I *am* spiritually fit, I don't need an answer. I just accept things as they are, right in that moment.

As Rhonda Findling writes in, "Be Free from Unhealthy Relationships" on the DailyOM website:

> I myself was going through a breakup when I wrote *Don't Call That Man!* as a way to work through my own feelings of anguish and loss over a relationship that didn't work out.
>
> As a result, I got published, which led to my building a successful private practice and the ability to leave

my job! Looking back that was a much better prize than that guy who I now realize was dysfunctional and emotionally unavailable.

Accepting, grieving, and finding gratitude in any situation is a skill requiring mindfulness and practice, but it works.

Gratitude—in every situation—is a powerful way to "judge with right judgment."

Dirty Laundry—Don't Judge by Appearances

An older couple had new neighbors move in next door. They watched to see what the new neighbors were like, but never went over to introduce themself.

One day, the wife remarked while looking out the kitchen window, "I don't think that new neighbor knows how to do laundry very well. The clothes on the line are still dirty."

Each week on the neighbor's wash day, the wife would criticize the neighbor's poor laundry habits, noting how filthy the clothes were, how sad the family must be having to wear dirty clothes, etc.

Her spouse rarely joined in but just grunted acknowledgment.

Then one day, the critical one exclaimed, "Well! I guess our neighbor must have learned how to wash clothes properly. Look! Their clothes are as clean as mine."

Her spouse looked up from the newspaper and said, "Honey, their clothes weren't the problem. They were always clean. I just washed our windows. Our windows were dirty."

Moral? Don't judge by appearances, but judge with right judgment. Remember, we rarely have all the information needed to make a right judgment. We have limited information and limited sight. Clean the windows of your mind. It doesn't matter how things are arranged, but instead, how our mind is arranged.

Change of Plans—Don't Judge by Appearances

When I retired early in 2015, I immediately resolved to spend the rest of that year consolidating my household finances, doing a lot of twelve-step recovery, resting and sleeping, adjusting to my new life, balancing my time, etc.

It was important to adjust and set a good solid foundation for this major life change. I took a slow and measured approach. I even did some part-time consulting for a not-for-profit to see if I liked it, to "taper off" from a regular work schedule.

My plan was to make 2015 a time to adjust to my new life. The next year, 2016, would be my year to travel. I had a long bucket list of things to do, places to see, and experiences I wanted to have.

I was fifty-seven years old and in reasonably good health. My HIV and diabetes were under control, and my addiction/alcoholism had been arrested for twenty-two years. By Christmas 2015, I was in good shape for 2016. Everything was going according to plan. Then....

I began having stomach pains and backaches. My daughters, Nicole and Robin, were visiting. Nicole had trained as a holistic healer, so she made some suggestions, but the pain got worse.

In early January, I went to see, my Network Chiropractor, Dr. Tracy Bloom. This method of chiropractic care uses energy, breathing, and "networking" between the healthy and any disconnected places in the body. Over many years, this healing modality has brought me out of physical crisis to stability and then into wellness.

That day in Dr. Tracy's office, I could not lie on my stomach on the chiropractic table. Dr. Tracy said, "Maybe it's appendicitis."

I hadn't thought of that. My great-grandfather had died of a burst appendix. He had refused to get it looked at right away. So, I didn't hesitate. I went straight to an emergency room.

A CT scan showed a mass in my abdomen. "On the pancreas," the attending physician said. He referred me to an oncologist, who—wrongly and prematurely—agreed it looked like pancreatic cancer, one of the most difficult cancers to treat. I was dismayed, but something deep inside told me I would be all right.

A very close friend, Mike Ridley, suggested I speak to another friend, a doctor who was an ovarian cancer specialist. I knew I didn't have ovarian cancer, but I called her that Sunday, and we talked for over an hour.

She said, "You don't have pancreatic cancer. With a mass that big, you would be very sick, losing two to three pounds a week, and be very weak. But you weigh 200 pounds and other than stomach pain, you're fine, healthy, and have good energy."

She knew the diagnosis was wrong over the phone! So I fired the first oncologist.

As an aside, one spiritual rule for me is that I insist that I must love my doctors, love my lawyers, love my accountant, love my therapist. I know these people have my best interest at heart. They are much more than mere functional professionals. They are an integral part of my spiritual treatment team.

Firing the first doctor opened the door for me to meet Dr. Stephen Wrzesinski, who was the head of oncology at a local hospital in Albany, New York, at the time.

After testing, Dr. Wrzesinski determined the mass was a cancer, but not pancreatic cancer. It was an enlarged lymph node that showed, after further tests, that I had Stage IV non-Hodgkins follicular lymphoma.

I wanted a second opinion, so he set me up at a famous Cancer Institute in Boston. My sister, Sue Frederick, went with me. The doctor there gave me a lot of encouragement and hope. I went back home and started my chemotherapy and immunotherapy.

On my first visit to the Infusion Center, my Unity minister, Rev. Crystal Muldrow, came with me. We took a few quiet moments to bless everything and everyone in the place, especially the chemotherapy chemicals in the IV bag.

As with my HIV medication experience, you may hear people say, "The cure is worse than the disease. The chemicals are poison. The side effects are worse than the cancer. The chemo-agents kill healthy cells. Etc." I ignored (or tried to ignore) all that talk. I looked past appearances and instead focused on the "truth."

All things work together for good for those who love God.

Remember: things are what we say they are. My dogs are neither cute nor scary.

We called the chemotherapy agents "life-giving healing juice." We blessed them. We affirmed that they were going to work perfectly, with no side effects whatsoever. We blessed the chair and the needles and the treatment nurses. We blessed the hell out of it, so there was nothing left but heaven!

Six months later, I rang the bell and walked out of there in remission.

I had planned to travel in 2016. Instead, the Universe sent me on another journey. I used Spiritual Prosperity and Abundance principles on this challenge. I looked and saw with right judgment.

I was pronoic! I asked to be shown how this challenge came to help, not hurt me. I reaffirmed again and again that lymphoma was not here to hurt me or mess with me. It was not bad luck; God did not roll the dice with my life.

I believed with faith that this was here to help me grow, to help me wake up. It came to help me show others there is nothing Spirit cannot handle, turning tragedy to triumph!

I was pronoic on steroids. I really found gratitude in this situation. I affirmed that I would be okay. I knew God was stronger than any diagnosis.

People said things like, "You were strong." I said, "No, I surrendered to win."

People said, "You fought cancer and beat it." I said, "No, I made friends with it."

Cancer helped me…. It did its job and then it went away once it had served its purpose.

The sudden change in my plans could have sent me into a spiral of self-pity, despair, and depression. I could've been demoralized, defeated, and dejected. No cancer diagnosis is welcome news. But whatever your situation, I am here to tell you, an attitude of gratitude will overcome any obstacle.

Get in the habit of judging, not by appearances but by right judgment. A powerful belief coupled with faith moves mountains.

Prosperity and abundance principles apply to all areas. Sowing seeds of positivity, joy, love, healing, hope, abundance, encouragement, zeal, happiness, peace, and life pays big dividends. We appreciate what we have, what comes, what is taken away, and what is left behind.

You Will Reap What You Sow, But….

You've heard it said, "We reap what we sow." Yes, we do reap what we sow, but not necessarily *where* we sow….

As I have said, we are highly attractive beings. It is a law of the Universe that says: What we do, say, think, believe, or feel sets up reverberations, vibrations, that shape the world we see and our lives. We sow seeds (ideas) in our minds and in the words we speak and the deeds we do. Those seeds sprout and grow, taking on lives of their own.

And we then reap the fruits of our thoughts, words, and deeds. However, we don't necessarily reap these rewards—consequences—directly. We may act negatively in one arena, and the vibrations we create can manifest repercussions in other areas.

For example, we may be stingy in giving out compliments to family members or coworkers. Good managers follow a rule: "Praise three times for every criticism." But we may do just the opposite. We may see lack in their behavior, and in our quickness to judge, point out shortcomings, or offer unasked-for advice.

The Truth Is: Unsolicited advice is really criticism in disguise.

In these ways, we sow seeds of mistrust and defiance, which will blow back later in the family or at work. That's reaping *where* we sow.

But this attitude can boomerang in other ways. We may karmically draw the boss who acts like us, critical and hard to please. The Universe always mirrors back what we ourselves are offering.

We may get a harsh and unfair review at work. We may encounter a traffic cop who seems biased and cruel. We may have a neighbor or a friend who becomes a busybody, nosy and intrusive.

Our energies have reverberations, and we cannot predict from where or just how they will come back in our direction.

We may have pilfered from petty cash or helped ourselves to office supplies, feeling a lack and "not enough-ness" in our workplace. Then "coincidentally" we lose a promotion we deserved. That is reaping *where* we sow.

But our fear and belief in scarcity that causes us to "save" a few pennies reflects a larger consciousness of limitations and lack that can show up in other places. Maybe we lose money on the street. Or an unexpected bill shows up. A hoped-for investment doesn't pay off, or we have other shortfalls and setbacks.

Remember, "To those who have, much will be given. But to those who have not, even that little will be taken away." If we feel and act like we have little, we will lose more. If we are happy and grateful for what we have, we tell the Universe we are open to receive more.

This law is powerful, and it works both ways. When we project feelings and words of truth, abundance, gratitude, compassion, and understanding, we will see those consequences. Life will flow easily. Our plans work out. Help comes at just the right time. An unexpected bill comes, and within days, an unexpected windfall comes in, mysteriously, just enough to cover the costs. We meet people we are supposed to meet who help us on our healing journey.

It has happened to me many times. Walking a spiritual path brings plenty of opportunities to grow. Next week, I will tell you a remarkable story of how I met an honest-to-God shaman and teacher, right outside my front door.

Finally, our positive, uplifting, attitude of gratitude radiates out and warms others. It changes people's moods and minds. We can be the ray of sunshine in someone's cloudy day.

A Course in Miracles says, "A miracle is never lost. It may touch many people you have not even met and produce undreamed of changes in situations of which you are not even aware." (Text-1.I.45)

Reaping in far-flung fields, generating miracles that assist people in far-off times and places can be understood by a phenomenon known as:

The Butterfly Effect

We don't know where, who, or how our ripples of healing light go out to touch others. However, a theory known as the Butterfly Effect helps explain it. This theory says that a butterfly's wings fluttering in the Amazon River basin can cause ripples in the atmosphere that, through a wholly and seemingly unrelated chain of events, cause a storm to develop in the Northern Atlantic.

This idea that small events can cause large effects in a system was first recognized by French mathematician Henri Poincaré and American mathematician Norbert Weiner.

In Spirit, seemingly inconsequential deeds can touch people and affect events far removed in time and space and in ways we will never know. It is a dramatic idea: We are so important, so powerful. It also makes us more mindful that even our simplest actions have consequences.

Remember, there are no idle thoughts. *A Course in Miracles* Lesson 16 reminds us that all thought creates at some level, making up our perception of the world. Thoughts produce actions, and this same phenomenon holds true.

Acting from our higher selves, we set in motion healing, enlivening energies. We generate hope, full of good possibilities. We sow seeds of peace and receive peace in return from a variety of sources, not just where we sow.

To have peace, we can search for it outside ourselves. We can demand that the world give us peace: tell the kids to be quiet, ask the boss to stop yammering, mute the television news, turn down the radio, shout at the jackhammer, block out the airplane overhead....

The world will never give us peace. We will not find it outside of us. We must cultivate it inside. Then the world responds to our highest and deepest thoughts and beliefs.

Do you want peace? *A Course in Miracles* offers this formula: To have peace, teach peace to learn it. (Text-6.V.B)

To have peace, joy, or love or any other thing of lasting value, offer it to another. Then you will *be* it.

Growing in prosperity consciousness, we will see no upward limit exists to our wealth, financial or otherwise. We are rich in health, rich in friends. We are overflowing with divine ideas, creative pursuits, joy, peace, and love. We have a growing fellowship of the spirit. We are in the fullness of life, happy and abundant, in reality and in our life's direction.

Remember, ideas are strengthened when shared. To increase peace, peace must be shared. Sharing spiritual ideas increases the idea in both the giver and the receiver. "We can only keep what we have by giving it away."

Even a small beginning, the smallest willingness, is enough to grow in abundance. We bless ourselves when we bless another and both are increased. The miracle seeds of our tiniest blessing to another will grow to become a tree that shades and feeds multitudes.

This is the lesson of the loaves and fishes: despite appearances, there is enough. There is more than enough. We have more than enough to share, and we are ready to receive even more abundance in all areas.

Limits of Believability

In Week 7, we spoke about believing in impossible things and exploring the limits of what we can believe. We touched on the process of imagination and putting wings to our dreams (taking action).

The limit of our belief is our horizon—the farthest we can see, envision, imagine. This belief takes effort, courage, and practice. Over time, we can stretch our beliefs to encompass new horizons, greater dreams, and deeper successes and triumphs.

Remember, belief activates faith! Our beliefs operate whether we are aware of them or not. We have been examining and bringing to the surface those deeply held beliefs to see if they are working for us or against us. We change those that do not serve us.

The following story illustrates how our beliefs can hold us back. Be aware and examine your beliefs. Then you can stretch your vision and have a full and prosperous life.

Limits of Our Horizon

> When the early Dutch settlers of New Amsterdam were reviewing their little settlement at the tip of Manhattan Island and planning for the future, they knew they were in a special place. They had plenty of water, land, and food, a natural harbor and more. They saw that more European settlers would come.
>
> They needed to plan for the settlement's growth. They commissioned a map to project the future street grid. They did their best to plan for the foreseeable future. They went to the edges of their sight, the very limits of their believability.
>
> They numbered the streets in a square grid making planning easy. When they finished, they believed they saw far enough into the future to accommodate the throngs who would soon arrive. They saw the settlement growing far past the boundaries of the village, so they stretched their limits of believability, north on Manhattan Island until they reached the farthest horizon they thought possible.
>
> 19th Street.

Yes! That was the limit of their sight: 19th Street! Some surely scoffed. The city couldn't grow that big! In those days Greenwich Village was wilderness.

Of course, anyone who knows New York City's street grid knows it goes all the way to 228th Street on Manhattan Island, and up to 263rd Street in the Bronx (a farm once owned by the Bronck family). Today's reality is amazingly distant from 19th Street, the limit to the settlers' realm of believability.

So, what is *your* 19th Street?

What are the limits of your realm of believability? Is it an income of $20,000 a year? Is your stretch $50,000 or $100,000? If you make $75,000, what is your 19th Street? Is it $200,000? A million?

Remember, your limit is only a fraction of your potential, a small possibility within a Universe of unlimited possibilities. Stretch yourself to the limit. See yourself as already there. Know there is good for you beyond your wildest imaginings.

Step 10—Continued to take personal inventory and when we were wrong, promptly admitted it.

Step 10 is simple, but it requires daily practice and willingness. We simply keep current by examining mistakes we've made and rectifying them promptly. In Steps 4 through 9, we cleaned house. Now it's a simple matter of doing daily housecleaning so things don't get out of hand—unmanageable—again. Small, frequent inventories keep our side of the street tidy. We want no messy situations festering, growing into larger problems that are difficult to put right.

The *Tao Te Ching*, Poem 64 says:

> *Prevent problems before they arise.*
> *Put things in order before they exist.*
> *The giant pine tree grows from a tiny sprout.*

We recognize and correct, early and frequently, the mistakes we make. The result is that we have more room, more energy to invest in productive and creative pursuits. We waste less energy on difficulties and easily avoided problems that can be nipped in the bud.

Step 10 is a way of life. Done sincerely, with willingness and practice, it is time well spent, a freeing habit that pays big dividends.

ACTION ITEMS
Work with Gratitude in *Everything*

See how Gratitude for difficult things frees your mind to see new possibilities and create more abundance. Find gratitude for the good stuff and the not-so-good-stuff. That is where gratitude becomes rocket fuel for a truly free consciousness that allows spirit to shine through the clouds.

Begin to Cultivate a 10th Step Practice

Take a daily inventory to check in and see how you've done and where you need to correct. Few activities are more profitable. If this step seems like a chore, try it for a while and see the results. They'll speak for themselves in increased freedom, and increased courage as we confront our minor mistakes and repair them right away.

Notice Where Your 19th Street Lies and Stretch!

What is the limit of your believability? How far do you think you can go in finances, career, relationships, freedom, travel, etc.? The limit of your mind is just that: your limit. It is not God's limit for you, so be ready to stretch and grow.

Reread Chapter 10 At Least Twice

Begin to Use This New Tithing Affirmation

I have enough!
I have more than enough!
I have more than enough to share!
And, I am ready to receive more!

Tithe*—Divine Love, flowing through me, blesses and multiplies all that I have, all that I give and all that I receive. We are blessed to know that Spirit is our Source. God bless! Thank you, God!*

Sing

    "I Am So Blessed"
    by Karen Drucker

    I Am so blessed
    I Am so blessed
    I Am so grateful, for all that I have
    I Am so blessed, I Am so blessed
    I Am so grateful, I Am so blessed

    We are so blessed
    We are so blessed
    We are so grateful, for all that we have
    We are so blessed, We are so blessed
    We are so grateful, We are so blessed

God bless! Thank you, God!

Week 11

Goals, Shamans, and the Mind of the Heart

*To pray is to descend into the heart,
and there stand before the face of the Lord,
all seeing within you.*

— Saint Theophan the Recluse

Goal Setting

A BIT MORE ABOUT goal setting. In Week 1, you picked a goal to manifest by the end of the course. Well, the end is in sight. Where are you on the path toward your goal?

Perhaps you've reached it already or it is close at hand. Perhaps it is failing to materialize, or by appearances, it seems to be blocked. We may appear stymied and far from our goal. Don't worry. Don't fear. Remember, we do not control "how" and "when" something will manifest. The Universe supplies the *how* and the *when*. Our job is to hold the vision, to ensure we are believing with faith.

Periodically take stock; review how we are doing on the road to our goal. Are we believing in something real and true, not fantasy or illusion? Have we done all we could, all the footwork? Are we seeing things right? Or trying to set things right?

This story helps illustrate how persistence in a true idea pays off.

Ted's Little Book

Once there was a man named Ted. Ted had written a book with his own illustrations. He loved and believed in his book. Ted lived in Connecticut and worked in New York City. On his lunch hour, he would take his manuscript and visit the publishing houses on Madison Avenue. For months, he showed his book to publishers, but nothing…his book was rejected, not once or twice, not three or four, nor a dozen times. Not eighteen times.

Ted brought his book to twenty-seven publishers. Twenty-seven separate publishing houses read his book, and twenty-seven editors rejected it. After the twenty-seventh rejection, he headed home discouraged, planning to burn his manuscript. Heading to the subway, he ran into a college friend, who had recently become an editor at Vanguard Press. He offered to read Ted's manuscript. He did, then took it to his senior editor who loved the story and the unique, quirky drawings. Vanguard agreed to publish Ted's book.

The rest is history. Ted was Theodore Geisel, who was introduced to the world as Dr. Seuss and went on to become wildly successful, writing more than sixty children's books. Geisel later said, "If I had been walking down the other side of Madison Avenue, I would be in the dry-cleaning business today."

The first Dr. Seuss book, *And to Think That I Saw It on Mulberry Street*, never would have been published had he not persisted past all failure…and if divine inspiration hadn't played a part in that chance meeting on Madison Avenue, just when Ted was about to quit.

Don't worry. Don't fret, stew, or doubt your goal. If it is a worthy goal, within your realm of believability, and you are doing your part, it *will* succeed! Don't give up on your goal, but you may have to give up: the human (ego) desire to fix, contrive, manipulate, barge ahead, force, or control.

Seek and Ye Shall Find

Siddhartha Gautama, born into a noble and wealthy family, saw poverty and misery everywhere outside of the family's luxurious compound. Vowing to find a solution to this suffering, he searched all the world for an answer. For six years he looked, traveled, tried… and failed. Discouraged, he gave up and sat under a fig tree—a Bodhi tree. There he remained, it is said, for forty-nine days. On the fiftieth day, he arose, enlightened….

Siddhartha, known from that day on as The Buddha, would not have achieved enlightenment had he sat under the tree on the first day of his search. He also likely would not have achieved enlightenment had he searched another six years.

The search was essential.

The surrender was also essential.

He didn't give up on his goal; he surrendered to the process. He stopped striving, controlling, pushing to succeed. He finally let go and success came.

Just like with Dr. Seuss, the effort must be accompanied by surrender, letting go of results. Then, and only then, can God come into the picture. We seek visible results, but we work in the realm of the unseen. The invisible. The realm of Spirit. We need to see with eyes of faith, not with our human eyes.

"I am rooted in the invisible" is one of my favorite affirmations. The physical world must be placed under the spiritual world.

> *"Peace I leave with you, my peace I give unto you: not as the world giveth, give I unto you. Let not your heart be troubled, neither let it be afraid."*
> — John 14:27

In Goal Setting, Let Spirit Lead You

Is your goal in your realm of believability? Is it really your heart's desire? Is it framed clearly? Have you done all you could, put all of your faculties into envisioning the goal, putting wings on your dream? Is anything important missing? Are you doing your part?

If the answer is, "Yes," then perhaps the missing ingredient is the surrender to Spirit, which allows the Universe to step in, completing the circuit, the cycle.

Whatever your goal, you can achieve it with patience, persistence, and faith. Your good is waiting for you. Make sure you have "eyes to see" clearly, first in mind and then in manifestation. Make sure you are allowing God to participate. Make sure you've balanced the "doing" with the "not-doing." Practice *Wu Wei*, which gives us more power and opportunity than we could ever have by ourselves.

In goal setting, having our eye on the goal is important, but it is equally important to pay attention to the big picture. Keep your eye on the horizon. Focusing on our spiritual path, we are not merely humans intent on getting stuff. We are spiritual beings, seeking awakening. Goals are signposts on our path, but our highest vision, our horizon, is really our guiding light.

Eye on the Plow?

In agrarian societies, most people tilled the soil to grow crops to feed themselves and their families. Many ancient spiritual texts like the *Tao Te Ching* and the Bible use farming analogies to illustrate spiritual matters. One such biblical saying of Jesus relates to goal setting: "No one who puts their hand to the plow and looks back is fit to enter the Kingdom of Heaven." (Luke 9:62)

This saying gives us a lesson in farming *and* in achieving spiritual goals. A good farmer wants to plow a straight furrow. To do so, one certainly cannot look backwards. That's foolishness. Spiritually, looking backward is a mistake if your purpose is to create a better future. Yet, you cannot look down at the plow either because the furrow will be crooked.

You can't even look down to the end of the field because, again, the line will not be straight. The only way to plow a straight line is to look past everything to the far horizon. Only then will the row be straight and true.

It's the same with your life and goals. You cannot achieve a goal by focusing solely on that goal; if you do, you will miss so much. Even when you achieve your goal, you likely will have "plowed a crooked furrow," ending up farther off the mark overall, in things like joy, serenity, love, and abundance.

We all know people so fixated on goals and ideas that their whole lives fall apart and they don't notice until it's too late. Single-minded obsession is the way of the fanatic, the mentally ill, and the addicted. A soft gaze on the far horizon lets us relax, trust, and see the bigger picture. Then we live looser, freer lives. We focus attention on the guiding, loving spirit of the Universe while keeping our goal in our peripheral vision. We enjoy the view and the journey.

Goal Setting—An Abundance of Goals!

We have been focused on a single goal for this course, but only by way of example. Living a truly abundant, prosperous life, we want to have many goals, in many areas: health, wealth, family relationships, creative endeavors, work/career, travel, friends, spiritual growth, annual income, etc.

In your abundance journal, start listing your goals. Call it a "Bucket List," "My Goals," "Things to Accomplish Before I'm [age]"... whatever. Write down all your goals, all your ideas.

Feel the excitement, using your imagination and all your senses, like a little kid writing a Christmas list for Santa. No idea is too big or too small.

Remember: Whatever you can conceive and believe, you can achieve!

Keep your list close by. Add to it. Cross things off as you achieve them, and pause to give thanks. Revel in your success. Don't just race on to the next thing. Remember: An attitude of gratitude is essential.

Share your success. My friend and therapist, Tony DelPozzo, says to do some "healthy bragging." It feels good, inspires others, and tells the Universe we are grateful. We are mindful of the blessings we have just been given.

Do your healthy bragging out loud. Set up a vibration of energy, excitement, gratitude, and possibility for future success. Show others what can be accomplished working together with the Spirit of the Universe!

We acknowledge our achievements and the Source from which all good things come. We do this with wild abandon and joy, knowing we are recipients of...

The Favor of God (Grace)

The Favor of God is an amazing thing. It is Grace. We mentioned this in a slightly different way in Week 6. Remember? "God makes his rain to fall on the just and unjust and his sun to shine on the righteous and the wicked."

The Truth Is: The "favor of God" is ours all the time. Unceasingly. Perfectly, in overflowing abundance.

A saying from the Middle East illustrates this: "The rain falls. In some places thorns grow, in other places, flowers. Yet the rain is the same."

Remember: We are children of the Universe, made of star stuff, and also remember, Spirit is capable of creating anything we desire.

Remember too: We are highly attractive, like magnets, pulling to us whatever we hold in consciousness. Knowing this, we can always attract to ourselves our highest and best good.

The favor of God—an unceasing flow of good to us from the Creator. In the stream of life, all good is available if we are ready, willing, and able to receive.

It is important to continually remember and remind ourselves: We are always receiving favor from the Universe. Seeing and acknowledging this is the height of gratitude, keeping our focus, not on appearances, but on right judgment.

The Truth Is: We are always praying.

When you pray, it is not begging for a favor; we pray in gratitude for what God has already given!

We can pray for favor for our loved ones and friends. It works. See God pouring out blessings upon your family, coworkers, friends, and acquaintances. This generates powerful energies for us and everyone we know.

"Thank You, God, for Thou hearest me. I know that you always hear me," Jesus said before praying to raise Lazarus from the dead.

This prayer came to mind for my friend Diane Albano when she read this section. She is a certified life coach, author of *The Art of Being Nice*, and one of the editors of this program.

Jesus was always confident that his prayers were heard, and we should be too as we learn to pray rightly, with faith.

Keep "in the flow of life," ready to receive your good, aware of the constant outpouring of abundance on everyone, everywhere. Our consciousness is forever being stretched, challenged to grow broader, deeper, and wider. We grow more capable to receive all the good that is ours. In this awareness, we begin to recognize and increase our...

Consciousness Capacity

> *"Remember, little flock. It is your Father's good pleasure to give you the kingdom."*
> — Luke 12:32

The benevolent Universe wants only the best for us. It is conspiring to make it happen. But we must cooperate and do our part. What's our part? To believe with faith! To hold in our minds and hearts true goals and ideas. To speak words of life.

As we practice, these ideas grow. We see our lives, our world, our minds change for the better. We increase our capacity to receive. This is why it is so important to tithe continually, faithfully, and joyously. To tithe in full expectation of our good coming to us. It is the most powerful action we can take to increase our spiritual muscles, to expand our capacity to receive.

Think of your consciousness as a spiritual container holding valuable things like ideas, love, abundance, wisdom, and healing light. You have a new wineskin (growing consciousness) to hold new wine (vibrant ideas of life).

What is your current capacity to hold the good God is flowing your way?

Leaky Dixie Cups vs. Tanker Trucks

What is the size of your consciousness? Paraphrasing Stretton Smith, in the 4T Prosperity Program for Abundance and the Fullness of Life: If God is pouring out a Niagara Falls of blessings upon you, and your consciousness is the size of a leaky Dixie cup, you won't be able to hold very much, will you?

There is a constant flow of joyous, riotous plenty being given freely and lovingly to everyone, everywhere, all of the time. This fact is the Law of Abundance. But we need a capacity to receive this good. We need to see it, acknowledge it, be grateful for it in advance of it manifesting. We must receive our good in full awareness that we are inheritors of the Kingdom of God.

This is the meaning behind Eric Butterworth's assertion that "God doesn't heal." Pretty blasphemous stuff, until you realize what he is saying: God is the healing itself—the love itself. It is our consciousness that needs to align with that healing flow of abundance.

How do we gauge our capacity to receive? One way is to look at your life. What is in accord—and what's out of alignment—with your highest good? Practicing the ideas in this program, wherever things are less than excellent, that's where your work lies.

Remember: Circumstances are not here to punish us. They are here to wake us up—to show us where gaps and character defects are, those places where thoughts of lack and limitation still hold sway.

When I was in elementary school, they taught us how to brush our teeth. They gave us little red dye pills. After you brushed your teeth, you dissolved the pill in your mouth. Your teeth would stain red wherever they were dirty, so you knew you missed those spots.

In our lives, the places where things are rough are our focus. Taking inventory in Steps 4, 5, and 10, we see where we fall short, where anxiety, worry, or regret linger—where we are stuck. These are the areas where we need work.

Also, look where we enjoy freedom, ease, and serenity. These "go to" places show us how well we're doing. These successes show how we worked with Spirit creating harmony, success, joy, abundance, and love.

When we are "in the flow of life," we notice and are grateful for the blessings constantly being poured out upon us. In this way, we experience...

Grace

"Grace" has been defined as "unmerited favor." We get grace just by being an integral part of the Universe. A child of God. This is the same as saying, "God makes rain fall on the just and unjust and the sun shine on the righteous and the wicked alike."

Grace does not rely on doing specific things. It does not depend on us tithing or being good to our neighbor or anything else we may do or fail to do. However, as we've said, those who follow spiritual laws and practice prosperity principles are more aware and more ready to receive God's grace, which is constantly pouring out.

Those "in the flow" can see God's gifts and accept them. Those not in the flow still receive grace, but they may not notice it, they may dismiss it, or they may receive it but not be grateful. They may take full credit rather than acknowledging their Source.

To be in a state of grace is to be in a state of love, joy, and gratitude. "Grace" and "gratitude" have the same root, from the Latin *gratus* meaning "pleasing, thankful." Recognize that we are given "all good things" freely and abundantly. Then we are ready to accept these gifts and are open to receiving more.

Truly, we are forever in a "state of grace." The only question is: Do we recognize it, acknowledge it, and act from it? Or does it pass us by because we don't have "eyes to see and ears to hear?"

Viktor Frankl, a famous psychiatrist who survived the horrors of the Holocaust, wrote in *Man's Search for Meaning*:

> We who lived in concentration camps can remember the men who walked through the huts comforting others, giving away their last piece of bread. They may have been few in number, but they offer sufficient proof that everything can be taken from a man but one thing: the last of the human freedoms—to choose one's attitude in any given set of circumstances, to choose one's own way.

That is a state of grace: to see past any appearances to a different reality, true and solid, the invisible rock upon which all things stand—love!

Frankl writes:

> For the first time in my life, I saw the truth as it is set into song by so many poets, proclaimed as the final wisdom by so many thinkers. The truth—that love is the ultimate and highest goal to which man can aspire. Then I grasped the meaning of the greatest secret that human poetry and human thought and belief have to impart: The salvation of man is through love and in love.

The Spirit of the Universe opens up a new road when we are stuck. When we are lost, our intuition presents an inspired idea or someone appears with a solution. We will often have powerful experiences of divine intervention.

My Friendly Neighborhood Shaman

Throughout the day, I would see the man who recently bought the house across the street from me in Albany, New York, walking his dog. Being a neighborly sort, I would say "Hello."

But he appeared not to hear me. I came to judge (by my mistaken perception) that he was *"the man who was a bit gruff."*

On a spiritual path, I tried new things to awaken and deepen my consciousness: workshops, lectures, meditation sessions, etc. Some things helped and some did not work for me. One avenue I wanted to explore was dreaming.

I heard of a man who led workshops and taught courses on using dreams for guidance and helping people dream bigger, deeper dreams. I found a number for him and called. The person who answered was nice, but said only people who had already worked with him were eligible to take classes and participate in retreats.

Hmm…. That door seemed closed.

Years later, I saw a flier advertising classes of all sorts: macramé, swimming lessons, how to do your taxes, etc. Among the offerings was an evening seminar on dreams and dreaming, offered by the dream teacher I'd tried to connect with years earlier. I signed up for the class.

The day before the evening course, my neighbor Pam called me. Pam never called me, so it was unusual. "Hi," she said, "I see you're going to Robert's class tomorrow. Do you want to ride with me?"

A nice offer, but I was curious. I asked how she knew I was going. "Oh, I help Robert plan his events, and I drive him, too. You can ride with us."

So that evening I got in Pam's car. We talked a few minutes. "Where do we pick up Robert?" I asked. "Oh, right here. He lives across the street."

Sure enough, a few minutes later, Robert Moss came out of his house across the street. My gruff neighbor!

He got in and we drove to the event. Robert couldn't have been nicer and more gregarious. We had the most interesting conversation and the workshop was fascinating. I bought two of his books, which he autographed, and he talked in a very animated and enthralling way all the way home.

Quite a difference from the person I had judged by appearances.

Robert Moss is an internationally known author, shaman, teacher, researcher, and expert on the history, mystery, and phenomenon of dreaming. He is intimately familiar with how people and whole societies use dreams to guide their lives, recover lost pieces of their souls, and awaken to infinite universes, realms, higher beings, and their own power and abilities to manifest healing, wholeness, and the life of our dreams.

"Wake up and dream!" is one of his slogans.

He was drawn to our little corner of the world after he began having nightly dreams in which an elderly woman, a shaman of a native tribe, spoke to him in a language he did not understand. Writing down phonetically whatever he remembered from his dreams, he showed it to various scholars. One recognized it as a variation of ancient Iroquois used by the Mohawks who lived in what is now Upstate New York.

"Island Woman" as the shaman named herself, was a medicine woman who was connected to an Irishman, Sir William Johnson, the British crown's Indian agent who was made a baronet after the Battle of Lake George in 1755 during the French and Indian War in the American Colonies.

Robert moved to the area to research and connect with the energies of this dreaming culture.

Since that first meeting, I have been privileged to do workshops and retreats with Robert, and help spread his message that dreams are important events, guiding us, warning us, showing us past and future selves (or selves who have parallel lives in other planes of the multiverse), helping people recover lost pieces of their soul through dream work/play.

On rare occasions, I have accosted him on the sidewalk to tell him a dream, always dreams which have "juice," aka power and resonance. He has been a friend, a guide, and mentor…this shaman I met outside my front door.

They say, "When the student is ready, the master will appear." I must not have been ready in those earlier years when I tried to connect with him. But the Universe knew I eventually would be, so the stage was set.

Just like my serendipitous start to my career in state government and politics, being "in the flow," when we "begin it now," people and resources appear, ones we could never have foreseen.

Remember this quote about what happens when we commit? "A whole stream of events issues from the decision, raising in one's favor all manner of unforeseen incidents and meetings and material assistance, which no man could have dreamed would have come his way."

Stay in the flow. Begin! Commit! See yourself in the stream, the Niagara Falls of God's good, God's abundance. Look for the hidden angels, helpers, guides, shamans, and even benevolent tricksters on your path. Nothing is here to hurt you. Pronoically, everything is on your side!

Step 11—Sought through prayer and meditation to improve our conscious contact with God, as we understood God, praying only for knowledge of God's will for us and the power to carry that out.

We seek power not for our own selfish interests (our ego) but to do God's will.

In Step 11, we seek to increase our reliance, our communication, and our awareness of God—and the power to do what we are meant to do. When we do our job, we will be fulfilling our most basic and our highest calling.

We are in a state of grace. We act out of pure Love, filled with joy and gratitude. We have all manner of support from beings both seen and unseen. We are given all the resources we need, to do whatever we are called upon to do. We are filled with freedom and purpose. We are a blessing to the world. We are seeing with eyes of faith; we are truly in the flow of life.

Prayer is not a rush of hurried words mumbled morning and night. Prayer is not begging a random Universe to do something it may or may not do.

The Truth Is: Prayer tells the Universe where our consciousness lies—and the Universe responds perfectly, in harmony with our current vibration.

Prayer is high-ordered thinking! Remember, effective prayer is *everything* we think, say, feel, believe, know, and do, all lined up in the same direction. That is a powerful prayer that brings results.

The Truth Is: Our whole life is one long, great, continuous prayer.

Viewing life through this lens (we are constantly praying, whether consciously or not), we can see clearly where we need to change, where the rough spots are, and where we are "on the beam," doing well and making progress.

Muddled and conflicted prayer brings us nothing we want and often hard lessons to help us change our minds (aka repent). Don't like what you're getting? Raise the vibration. Change your mind. Think a new thought; then act upon it.

Ask for help. If you don't know what to do, stop and ask—and the answer will come, if your own spiritual house is in order. Remember, "God speaks to me all through the day," from *A Course in Miracles*. That is where meditation comes in.

We pray by aligning...everything. We meditate by getting still and listening.

We still our thoughts, our bodies, our doubts to listen for the "still, small voice," the voice that doesn't shout, insist, or bully. It gives, with gentle, loving care, all we need, guiding and directing us, seeing the big picture with all the information.

And prayer is inside of us all the time.

Denials, affirmations, and gratitude are front and center here. Dust off that mirror you were using in earlier weeks. See yourself. Repeat with power and certainty.

Denials... This is not true.

Affirmations... T*his* is wholly true.

Gratitude... I am so happy and grateful now that [blank].

This is the way to pray, changing our minds, thoughts, and inner life. Our mind shifts and our outer world shifts in response. Denials, Affirmations, Gratitude. Our life as prayer. It is vital that we not just *think* the Universal Truths we have been discussing. We need to...

Say Them Out Loud!

Just a friendly reminder that our voice speaks a vibration that activates and harmonizes with the vibrations of the Universe. Speaking Words of Life aloud produces effective denials, affirmations, gratitude, and prayers, and ultimately, the desired result.

God didn't think, "Let there be Light." God *spoke* the activating words aloud.

Hearing our voice vibrating in our chest, vocal cords, mouth, and tongue, our words pour out into the air vibrating molecules. The sound waves radiate out into the world as we proclaim with certainty and power our truth—The Truth!

Speak the words of life that will change your mind, and thereby, change your life.

Mind of the Heart

Stretton Smith in the 4T Prosperity program tells of the nineteenth century Theophan the Recluse, Bishop of Tambov, Russia, and a well-known Russian Orthodox saint. Theophan spent his whole life meditating on an idea that can be summed up as, "Put your mind in your heart and love God."

We transfer our conscious thought from the head (ego) to the heart (spirit). Theophan's idea takes practice and more practice, but it is attainable.

To feel our conscious thoughts, feelings, and beliefs shift from a head-centered perspective into a heart-centered perspective is quite profound. Theophan wrote:

> Descend with your attention into the heart, stand there before the Lord and admit nothing sinful to enter there. Attention to that which transpires in the heart and proceeds from it—this is the chief activity of the proper Christian life.

When I go into prayer or meditation, I place my hand gently near my heart, grounding my attention and energy there. I repeat these words: "I am centered within the consciousness of my heart."

Take time to pray and meditate, using the heart-centered energy that heals. In that space, we slow down and become mindful.

Mindfulness and Slowing Down

"Slowing down also lets you be more mindful, deliberate, and fully present. When we slow down, we are giving ourselves the opportunity to reacquaint ourselves to our natural rhythms. We let go of the 'fast forward' stress and allow our bodies to remain centered

> *and grounded. Slowing down is inherent to fully savoring anything in life."*
> — Madisyn Taylor, *Doing Things Slowly* in DailyOM

Practice helps us to go inward and hear the still small voice, find a good orderly direction (GOD), and settle into a higher groove, a higher energy vibration.

When we manifest a higher level from a slower vibration, we bring more space into our minds and hearts. We have more time to act—rather than react—and remember our spirit's connection to source.

Prayer for Ourselves and Others:

Unity Prayer for Protection
The light of God surrounds us;
The love of God enfolds us;
The power of God protects us;
The presence of God watches over us;
Wherever we are, God is!
And All is Well!

Prayer for Others:
Child of Light
Child of Light, I Bless you,
I think of you, I pray for you,
Not in terms of what I think you need,
Or what I think you should do or be or express.
I lift up my thoughts about you.
I catch a new vision of you.
I see you as a child of light.
I see you guided and directed by an inward Spirit that
leads you unerringly into the path that is right for you.
I see you strong and whole;
I see you blessed and prospered;
I see you courageous and confident;

I see you capable and successful.

I see you free from limitation or bondage of any kind.

I see you as the spiritually perfect being you truly are.

Child of Light, I bless you.

— From Unity's *Daily Word*, May 18, 1975[4]

ACTION ITEMS

Continue to review your goal for the course

See what is next to do. See where you are and make sure your goal is still in alignment.

Create your "Bucket List" of goals

Have fun with this! Create many goals in all areas. That is one key to a consciousness of abundance. It creates joy and excitement. It creates a true sense of possibility. It allows us to reinforce our worthiness. "I can have it all!"

Expand and expand. Add more goals so you have goals in all areas: spiritual growth, education, health, wealth, family and friends, relationships, work, hobbies, travel, creative pursuits, etc.

Examine your "consciousness capacity."

Where is yours? Broaden, deepen, and expand it.

In *The Artist's Way*, Julia Cameron talks about how having an unlimited God is like having an unlimited bank account. We can draw on it and draw on it, and it is never exhausted. But we most often cheapen and diminish God by our feelings of unworthiness and small thinking, when (paraphrasing), "It is God's good pleasure to give us the kingdom."

Practice Step 11, prayer and meditation

Speak your denials, affirmations, and gratitude aloud. Feel the energies. Feeling is so important to imagination, in gratitude, in shaking off old tired ways, with the excitement that something newer and better is ours for the asking—with some sweat and perseverance, of course.

---

[4] Reprinted with permission of Unity®, publisher of Daily Word®.

Like most things, this is a lifetime discipline. We get better at it as we gain experience using it. Don't be like me, who never practiced the piano because I wasn't good at the piano. That was my old, childish thinking. You only get better by practice. Then, what was once difficult becomes easy and there are more challenging lessons to master.

Reread Chapter 11 At Least Twice

Use This New Tithing Affirmation

I have enough!
I have more than enough!
I have more than enough to share!
And, I am ready to receive more!

Tithe—*Divine Love, flowing through me, blesses and multiplies all that I have, all that I give and all that I receive. We are blessed to know that Spirit is our Source. God bless! Thank you, God!*

Sing

"I Am So Blessed"
by Karen Drucker

I Am so blessed
I Am so blessed
I Am so grateful, for all that I have
I Am so blessed, I Am so blessed
I Am so grateful, I Am so blessed

We are so blessed
We are so blessed

We are so grateful, for all that we have
We are so blessed, We are so blessed
We are so grateful, We are so blessed

God bless! Thank you, God!

Week 12

Your Spiritual Awakening

*I slept and dreamt that life was joy.
I awoke and saw that life was service.
I **acted** and behold, service was joy.*
— Rabindranath Tagore (Gurudev)
(emphasis added)

"Follow your inner moonlight; don't hide the madness."
— Allen Ginsburg

Step 12—Having had a spiritual awakening as the result of these steps, we tried to carry this message to others and to practice these principles in all our affairs.

WHAT A MOUTHFUL. What an order. This step has so much to ponder...and so much to do.

Having had a spiritual awakening as the result of these steps...

Step 12 assures us that we have had a "spiritual awakening."

If we have made a sincere effort over the past eleven weeks to do the work and follow the steps, we will have had a spiritual awakening—or at least the beginnings of one. You can be assured that your awakening will unfold, deepen, and grow as you continue doing your prosperity work.

What is a spiritual awakening? The simplest explanation is we have had an inner change, mentally, emotionally, perhaps physically.

We can look back to Week 1 and see where we were and where we are now. We can see how far we've come.

Simply put, we have begun to change our minds (repent). Our thinking has started to shift, and our outer life has, and will continue to, shift as well.

A Course in Miracles defines a miracle as a shift in perspective. Our perception shifts and things do not look the same. Outside, perhaps nothing has changed, but *inside*, things look different, and so they *are* different.

Einstein said, "The greatest power in all the universe lies within one's ability to change their mind."

Furthermore, quantum physics shows us that our physical world is a reflection of consciousness. We are what we think. The world is what we think it is.

All ancient spiritual wisdom rests on this foundation:

- Correct your mind, and your life will fall into place. (Lao Tzu)
- As a man thinketh in his heart, so he is. (Proverbs 23:7)
- Anything is possible for him who believes. (Mark 9:23)
- Life is Consciousness. (Emmett Fox)
- So, direct your face toward the Path, inclining to truth. Adhere to the Nature of Allah upon which He has created humanity. No change should there be in the creation of Allah. That is the correct Path, but most of the humanity do not know. (*Quran*, Surah Ar-Rum 30:30)

All religions and spiritual traditions share the same goal: to bring our human consciousness up and away from the material world, expanding our minds until they are One with God-Mind.

"Having had a spiritual awakening" means our thoughts have shifted to a higher order—our prayers are less mumbled words and more integrated.

Even so, and despite our hard work and willingness, perhaps certain situations have not been resolved; they are the same or even a bit "worse" (as judged by appearances). Perhaps we have not yet reached the goal we set for ourselves.

All of these are externalities. Important, but the change we look for is inside of ourselves.

- Perhaps we handled a situation differently and better than we used to.
- Perhaps we didn't handle it better, but we *noticed* our behavior and it didn't feel right.
- Perhaps we faced a fearful situation and survived and felt the rush of courage and accomplishment afterward.

We don't get courage to face a fearful situation. We face a fearful situation and receive courage as a reward, to help us face the next situation."

- Perhaps we are more at ease and at peace.
- Perhaps we feel freer than we did twelve weeks ago.
- Perhaps we smile more.
- Perhaps we've taken on new projects, found new support, made new friends.
- Perhaps we hear the "still, small voice" for the first time, or hear it more often, more clearly, with more certainty.
- Perhaps we trust our gut, our intuition more. We listen and then act on our intuition, even when what we're told to do doesn't seem logical, and we see that the situation played out better than we could have hoped.

These are just a few examples of what a spiritual awakening may look and feel like.

This is a mere beginning. There is more to come with practice, patience, and persistence.

The Truth Is: Infinite, limitless expansion is a hallmark of the Universe.

There is no limit to the upward growth you can achieve, no constraints upon the ease and freedom you can enjoy.

Your spiritual awakening will come about through action, from doing the work, from the steps, and from practicing your spiritual principles of abundance, tithing, and gratitude, using affirmative prayer, goal setting, internal house-cleaning, and the rest.

With this awakening comes the responsibility to maintain and increase your consciousness of abundance. You must try to help others, and continue to practice these spiritual principles in all areas of your life.

...we tried to carry this message to others (aka Service)

Step 12 asks us to help others discover these principles. Helping to heal others, freeing them from fear and lack, is crucial to your success and growth. This spiritual principle is exactly the same as tithing: whenever, whatever you give, you receive in direct measure, and even more.

> *"One's arms and hands are to be thought of, and used, as God's arms and hands, the expression of God's-mind ideas of power and living service and splendid work."*
> — Myrtle Fillmore, *Healing Letters*

> *"The best way to find yourself is to lose yourself in the service of others."*
> — Gandhi

In giving, while mindful of spiritual principles, remember you are no longer subject to the world's rules. The old idea that someone gains and someone loses is no longer in effect. You now operate under higher laws. Giving, you really give to yourself.

In giving, both giver and receiver are blessed and increased.

> *I have enough*
> *I have more than enough.*
> *I have more than enough to share.*
> *And I am ready to receive more.*

The Truth Is: You can only keep what you have by giving it away. This twelve-step recovery slogan is powerful. It is true for ideas, for spiritual principles, and for spiritual energies, like money or love.

It is true for money because money is an idea. It is true for love because we are made of love, and exchanging love increases love in you, in others, and in the world.

The world says there are givers and takers, winners and losers. Spirit says there is only oneness and love; there is only abundance.

A Course in Miracles Lesson 108 says, "To give and to receive are one in Truth."

Profound but simple: All is one, so I give from myself, to myself.

Your gift (an idea) is given and received. It is strengthened and increased in both the one who receives and in the one who gives!

Taking care of yourself in a healthy, non-selfish, non-egotistical way, you help others to find the freedom and the responsibility to take care of themselves. You show them they can do it. Shining your light, you give others light by which they can see.

Offering increase to those who temporarily have less shows others they are worthy and loved. This gives them the space they need to start their own healing.

Generosity should not descend into enabling, but gifts to those who have less—money, hope, encouragement, relief, understanding, or compassion—are definite forms of service. Service to others is something the world says is a chore, an inconvenience. But Spirit says it is a doorway to awakening innumerable gifts.

The Popular Story of the Bodhisattva

This story is a lesson in compassion and service. It helps us to know and remember: If one suffers, we all suffer.

> The myth tells that the lovely, androgynous saint, a Bodhisattva, was on the verge of entering into nirvana, leaving behind forever the world of samsara (the world of delusion and suffering). Just as the meditation was deepening and insight into the transience of all phenomena was growing, the Bodhisattva was distracted by a great groaning, rising up all about in the world.
>
> Now out of the trance and looking around, the saint asked: "What is this groaning I hear?" All the birds and trees and grass and all sentient beings replied:
>
> "O, Bodhisattva, your presence here among us has given us joy and a reason for living. We all love you so, and we are saddened by the prospect of your leaving us. And so, we groan."
>
> Filled with compassion, the saint vowed to renounce nirvana until all sentient beings were equally enlightened.

Service to others is vital to our continued spiritual growth, to increase prosperity consciousness and joy in ourselves and in others. It reminds us we give to ourselves when we give to others.

> *"Whatsoever you did for the least of our sisters and brothers, you did for me."*
> — Matthew 25:40

Share your light! Uncover, discover, and recover your passions, your talents, your desires, and your dreams. Share your gifts with the world so that all beings may become enlightened.

To do this, we must become completely who we are in truth. Shakespeare said in *Hamlet*, "To thine own self be true." These powerful spiritual principles will remove all the old ideas, the false beliefs, the dysfunctional patterns that are blocking our light.

The *Tao Te Ching*, Poem 15 says:

> *Do you have the patience to wait*
> *'Till your mud settles and the water is clear?*
> *Can you remain unmoving*
> *'Till the right action arises by itself?*

In other words, removing all of what is "not you," what's left is the true you whom God has created, free from fear, lack, neediness, and the other character defects we've discussed.

Oscar Wilde said, "Be yourself; everyone else is already taken."

To do service, to give and receive in the way of Spirit, to truly be who you are is an amazing journey full of promise and a lifetime of discovery.

A story from China may help illustrate.

The Stonecutter's Wish

> A lowly stonecutter toiled each day in the quarry, chipping at the granite with hammer and chisel until great slabs of the mountainside fell away.
>
> Chip-chip-chip. It was dusty, boring work. The stonecutter wished to be someone, anyone, other than a lowly stonecutter.

One day, the governor of the province came along the road in a fine sedan chair with a large entourage. The stonecutter saw them and said, "Oh, I wish I could be the governor! That would be a fine life. Governors are very powerful."

In an instant, the wish was granted, and the stonecutter was bumping along in the ornate sedan chair, carried by the governor's bearers. The stonecutter was pleased and amazed. "This is the life!"

Unfortunately, the stonecutter did not know that the governor was headed to the palace of the emperor, who was very angry with the governor. They arrived and the poor stonecutter was dragged before the emperor. Suddenly, this was not such a good life after all.

"Oh, I do not want to be the governor. This is terrible. But emperor, now that is something. I wish I were the emperor." And—poof!—the stonecutter sat on the emperor's throne, yelling at the trembling governor.

"This is more like it! The emperor is truly the most powerful being on earth," thought the stonecutter.

That afternoon, the emperor traveled out to a distant province. As the caravan made its way, the sun beat down on them and was very hot. It was miserable, dusty, and uncomfortable. The sun was merciless.

"Oh, this is no good. The emperor cannot be more powerful than that blazing sun. Ah! But if I was the sun, then I would be most powerful and most comfortable. I wish I were the sun." And—poof!—the wish was granted. Now the stonecutter was the blazing sun.

The stonecutter had fun for a time, shining brightly here and there, becoming hotter, so people had to put on hats and take off their cloaks. But then a cloud came by. It blocked the sun, so the sun couldn't shine on the people anymore.

"This is no fun. The sun isn't as powerful as a little cloud? I don't want to be the sun if I can't do what I want. But that little cloud seems to be more powerful than the sun. I wish I were a cloud." And—you guessed it—the lowly stonecutter was now the cloud.

The cloud had a good time blocking the sun, making people take their hats off and put their cloaks back on. Even making a little rain was amusing. Until a great wind came blowing, shredding the cloud into wisps....

"A wind can be more powerful than a cloud, which can be more powerful than the sun? I don't like this game at all. Since the wind is most powerful, I wish I were the wind." No sooner said than done, and the stonecutter was a giant gust of wind, blowing to-and-fro across the land.

Now hats and cloaks were flying everywhere! This was great fun, and the stonecutter knew this was it.... Until....

The wind slammed into a giant wall. What? It was a mountain, tall and solid. It blocked the wind completely. There was no getting around or over it.

"Sigh! Even the wind meets its match. I do not want to be the wind if I can't blow everywhere and anywhere. This mountain is more powerful than the wind. I guess I will be the mountain." And immediately the stonecutter felt solid and tall and immoveable. The wind beat against the sides but to no avail.

Finally, at peace, the stonecutter relaxed, satisfied and happy. "I am finally the most powerful thing there is. Nothing can have any effect on my majestic mountain-hood."

The stonecutter's happy repose was profound and complete. Until....

Far below, the stonecutter-mountain heard a faint noise.

Chip-chip-chip. Gazing down from on high, the sound got clearer. Looking closely down at the very foot of the mountain, the stonecutter saw....

A lowly little stonecutter chipping away in the dusty quarry.

The moral, of course, is: Be what you are. We each have singular talents, a purpose, what we are meant to be and what we are called to do. Don't look outside of yourself for happiness. It is already there inside. To give of our gifts, fulfill our part in Creation, we release all that we are not, to let God's light shine through us in our clarity and stillness.

Lesson 97 in *A Course in Miracles* is:

> I am spirit.
>
> Today's idea identifies you with your one Self. It accepts no split identity, nor tries to weave opposing factors into unity. It simply states the truth...[that] will bring your mind from conflict to the quiet fields of peace. No chill of fear can enter...letting go of illusions of a split identity.
>
> We state again the truth about your Self, the holy [child] of God who rests in you, whose mind has been restored to sanity.

Note the implicit reference to Step 2. Being restored to sanity means knowing completely who and what we are!

Then, *A Course in Miracles* Lesson 98 gives us our marching orders:

> I will accept my part in God's plan for salvation.
>
> Today...we take a stand...we side with truth and let illusions go.... We dedicate ourselves to truth today and to salvation as God planned it. We will not argue it is something else. We will not seek for it where it is not. In gladness, we accept it as it is and take the part assigned to us by God.
>
> How happy to be certain...! We have a mighty purpose to fulfill and have been given everything we need with which to reach the goal.

...and to practice these principles in all our affairs.

"We will not seek for it where it is not." Which is to say, outside of ourselves, outside of God, outside in the world, in material things, in money, property, or prestige. We cannot stress enough that the act of tithing tells our inner self, and the Universe, that we know where our safety and security lie.

The simple act of tithing makes it infinitely easier to put God first and to practice these principles in all our affairs. This part of Step 12 is easily understood, but perhaps a bit harder to apply, easier in some areas than in others. But this is the very heart of *Prosperity Now!*

We have emphasized that money is our vehicle, but we know true prosperity is infinitely more than just money.

In Week 1, we listed areas where we would like improvement, ease, abundance, and growth. Step 12 tells us to practice the spiritual principles in every aspect of our life—another lifetime endeavor, but one that holds infinite promise.

Watch as your interior consciousness and the exterior garden of your life flourish! When you sow seeds of generosity, patience, courage, faith, love, serenity, peace, joy, happiness, zeal, excitement, and more into your work, families, friendships, hobbies, leisure time, daily routines, etc. all good things will increase beyond your wildest dreams.

We give a blessing. We receive a blessing. We *are* a blessing.

When we practice these principles in all areas of our lives, we are shedding old, stale thinking and seeing things with new eyes. Our faith is stronger than ever. Situations that would have thrown us off track in the past, we now handle with ease, grace, and magic, because we are pronoic and we see it right.

People wonder what has gotten into us.

They wonder when we became "rich."

They ask themselves (or gossip to others) how is it that we are able to do such fantastic things.

They wonder how we seem to get younger looking.

They ask what's our secret.

They may become a little envious or even jealous.

That's okay. With love, grace, a little patience, and compassion, we help each other by shining our light so others may see, not in an egotistical, angry, or inappropriate way but in a way that radiates joy and peace and power.

> Quit letting negative comments upset you. They wouldn't be talking about you if you weren't making a difference. Nobody talks about people who aren't doing anything, that don't have any influence. They're talking about you because you're going places. They can see there's something special about you. You have the favor of God. — Joel Osteen

People will watch us grow and prosper, change and adapt, and they want what we have. Are they willing to do the work and stick to it as you are doing? People see the success, but they often don't see or acknowledge the sweat and effort that went into it.

The Truth Is: It takes twenty years to become an overnight success.

Step 12's directive to carry the message to others while practicing these spiritual principles in every aspect of your life is the summation of everything we've talked about.

And the beauty is, in tune with intuition, the "still, small voice," you will do it naturally, without forethought, contrivance, or manipulation. Opportunities will arise to practice, and you will rise to meet the occasion.

> *"Do not worry about how to respond or what to say. In that hour you will be given what to say. For it will not be you speaking, but the Spirit of God speaking through you.*
> — Matthew 10:19-20

Think about this quote whenever you are called on to offer the opening prayer or confront an angry customer.

All Means All

You recall from Week 1 that prosperity and abundance are more than just material wealth. Wealth is a long list of things and shows up in many places:

- A functional loving family
- An abundance of good friends
- Joyous employment or other productive activities

- Good physical, mental, and emotional health
- A spirit of generosity
- Peace of mind (serenity)
- Healthy, healing laughter
- Altruistic intent to create a better world
- An abundance of love from Source—and from the many channels of supply

Then you were asked to add your ideas of what a prosperous, abundant, full life looks like:

_____

_____

_____

_____

Has your thinking changed over these twelve weeks? What did you list in Week 1? What would you list now?

Your springboard for these Spiritual ideas—Spiritual Laws—has been primarily centered around tithing and money, not to increase material wealth *per se*, but to use the difficult arena of finances to achieve growth in "all our affairs."

Health is one area even more fraught with anxiety than money. Telling people their thinking causes their physical difficulties is a dicey business. A fine line exists between "blaming the victim" and the resultant spiritual malpractice of chiding people for not "thinking affirmative thoughts" and proclaiming the truth.

The Truth Is: You are not a victim of the world you see.

A Course in Miracles Lesson 31 states:

> I am not the victim of the world I see.
>
> Today's idea is…your declaration of release…. It is a declaration that you will not yield to [any form of error-thinking] and not put yourself in bondage.

Replace all thoughts of error-thinking. Realize that God is in your mind and everywhere you look. When you see Divine Order in the midst of chaos, when you see the "new thing" God is doing, the new thing which is being born while the old system is breaking down; when you see the truth of your infinite capacity for health and wholeness despite appearances, you will remember you are not subject to the world's laws any longer.

You are not a victim once you claim your complete worthiness—your birthright as a child of God. When you see the world through eyes of faith, you will grow in confidence. As you master the spiritual principles of prosperity and abundance, you will see the world with a new perspective.

Remember, we see the world, not as it is, but as we are. Also, life is not having more, so we can do more, so we can be more.

The Truth Is: Life is not having more, to do more, so we can be more.

Life is *being* more. Then we can do more. Then we will have more. In other words....

Life Is Lived from the Inside Out

The world has things backwards. Experiences do not come upon us from outside. Life is not happening to us. That is a victim mentality.

Instead, our outer life reflects our inner state of mind. Life happens from us, in us, through us, and for us.

Life, change, and growth always happen from inside out. If you want to change your outer circumstances, change your inner landscape, your thinking and beliefs.

The miracle is the perspective shift. Inside is where to focus your attention. No matter what the outer world is presenting, resist your natural, human tendency to try to fix the outer—to set it right.

Your job is to *see* it right. Mind is the problem, and mind is the solution. Mind (spirit) is the only reality that really is.

What Is Moving?

Two students of the master were having an argument while walking along the temple grounds. They were looking at a pennant flying high above the towers.

"It's the flag moving," one insisted. "You can plainly see the flag is moving. There is no debating that. The flag is moving."

"No," the other countered. "I see that the flag is being blown by the wind, so it is not the flag that is moving. Flags cannot move. It is the wind. Wind is moving."

The master came by at that moment and was accosted by both students. "Which of us is right?" they demanded to know. "Is the flag moving, or is it the wind that is moving?"

She looked sternly at them. They should know better! "Flag not moving. Wind not moving. Mind is moving!" the master exclaimed and walked on.

Keep in mind (pun intended) everything exists in the mind. The more you can focus inwardly, the less you will be blown about by outside forces. The more you know yourself and remember that your perspective shift is the miracle, the more you will be at peace.

Remember, God does not heal. Your consciousness directly aligned with God-Mind is how healing happens.

Looking inside to your inner landscape, you will see how an event, person, situation, problem, concern, fear, setback, etc. is helping you to awaken. These outside events mirror back something inside that needs adjusting or removing.

As you grow in your prosperity, making changes and developing new awareness, new levels of faith, it is important to continually "check in" on your thinking and feeling.

Remember, your comfort zone (nice, but where little learning happens) and your panic zone (dangerous and also where little learning happens). Stay as long as you can in the learning zone, where you grow in mastery, even though it is often uncomfortable.

The unfamiliar learning zone will in time become your expanded comfort zone. Stretching your consciousness to a higher level of prosperity, what was once uncomfortable will now be inside your comfort zone.

So, Where Is My Prosperity Comfort Zone?

An easy way to gauge your prosperity comfort zone is to take a day and go to different places that, to you, represent various levels of "wealth" or opulence. At each place, check in with yourself. How does each one feel? Department stores are good places to do this, as are big city hotels or perhaps nearby neighborhoods.

Throughout this exercise, tune in to your inner landscape. Above all, do not judge yourself; just notice your thinking and feeling. Make note of any old messages and tapes that may be triggered.

Take yourself to a discount store. Walk around. Look at the people. Feel the vibe. Notice the energy. How does this feel? Do you feel comfortable? Out of place? Does this place reflect who you are?

Next, head to a mid-range store, something a bit more upscale but not fancy. Again, take note of the surroundings, and then take note of how you respond to the location. Is this place you?

Then walk into a luxury store, one where the prices are clearly beyond your present means. How does this feel? Notice the people who frequent this store. Do they seem at home? Do you seem at home?

Sit in the lobby of a luxury hotel and watch what goes on. Observe the outer, but really pay attention to the inner. Are you in the comfort zone? The panic zone? Is this place you?

There is an upscale outdoor shopping center near my hometown. I used to avoid it. It was not me. Too tony. Too chic. Not my kind of stores, not my kind of people.

That was then. But for many years now, it has been my favorite place to go to walk the dogs, especially in inclement weather because of its covered sidewalks. I like the atmosphere, the restaurants, and the shops. I am now comfortably at home there.

Remember, our course is not about manifesting more money, but about raising our level of prosperity consciousness. How we feel in low-, medium-, or high-end establishments is a guide to our inner thoughts about worthiness.

Clearly, I am not saying I need to stay at the Waldorf Astoria to feel worthy. I am saying that I already feel worthy. I felt so worthy back then that staying at the Waldorf Astoria was within my realm of believability. Today, it is solidly in my comfort zone.

Yet, at one time, it was in my panic zone.

The Waldorf Salad Experience

Stretching out of your comfort zone takes effort, but it also takes consciously and consistently remembering that your Higher Power is on your side and is ready, willing, and able to bring you your highest good and support your deepest dreams and desires.

Remember: When you "Begin it now!", all manner of resources come into play to assist you.

When I first started doing prosperity work with my teachers, I used their suggestion: Have many goals. I made a very long bucket list. One item was to eat Waldorf Salad at the Waldorf Astoria. Not long after, I decided to take some family to see a Broadway show. I found discount tickets and planned to go on a discount hotel website.

Booking the tickets, the website suggested adding a hotel package. I looked at the hotels they offered. Lo and behold! There was the Waldorf Astoria at a reasonable price, so I booked it. I felt so elated. I would fulfill one of my bucket list items.

Arriving in the grand lobby, we saw the famous nine-foot-tall, bronze-and-mahogany clock tower, which is topped off by Lady Liberty, a gift from Queen Victoria to America, which was first exhibited at the 1893 Chicago World's Fair!

I went to check in. The desk clerk looked at the computer and said, "Oh! You're not in the hotel. You're in the Waldorf Towers." He pointed across the grand lobby to a small side door.

As we trundled off, I was disappointed and disturbed. No wonder the price was so cheap. They put us in an annex. The appearances were clear. The small door led to a small, dingy hallway, at the end of which was another small door and a small desk.

I told the attendant my name. He checked his list and escorted us to the elevator to take us to our room on the twenty-fourth floor. As we rode up, I told him my story and my disappointment. "I figured it was too good to be true."

"Well," he said, "these are the towers. They put overflow guests here when the hotel is full. These are the residences."

That information did not sink in…until we arrived on our floor and walked down a sumptuous hallway to a door that opened onto an apartment larger than my modest brownstone row house in Albany.

This spacious apartment had a galley kitchen, huge living room, many windows, a large bedroom, and a sunken sitting room that went down into a large bathroom. The lap of luxury for a modest price, a rate quite a bit cheaper than an average hotel room in New York City.

And the next day for lunch, I got my Waldorf Salad.

You might just notice the sublime humor of the Universe. The appearances were easily judged—meager and low-grade. The hallway was dingy. The door off the grand lobby looked as if it could have easily led into a broom closet.

Judging by appearances was my first reaction. The beautiful blessing was beyond the sight of my physical eyes. Had I "judged with right judgment," I might have known that whatever was up ahead was for my highest and best good and for those around me as well.

Another New York City Hotel "Bucket List" Story

I always wanted to go to see the Macy's Thanksgiving Day Parade. However, you have to book parade-view rooms a year or more in advance. So, I booked a room in a hotel on the parade route but on the other side of the hotel. My daughters were coming into the city to see the parade with me.

I had just settled into my room when suddenly the door opened. A woman stood there with luggage and a key. "This is my room!" she declared.

"No, it's mine," I said. "I just arrived. My key worked."

She explained she had booked this room, which was across from her sister and her children. Rather than get defensive (panic zone), I invited her in, and I called the front desk. They had made a mistake. A bellhop would be up shortly. They would give me another room.

I wasn't happy, but I was glad they had another room for us. I chatted with the woman until the bellhop came. He took me to a higher floor and my new room—which overlooked the Thanksgiving Day parade route—a rare and difficult thing to come by. My parade-route room had been manifested. Thank you, God!

My daughters arrived and we had a marvelous Thanksgiving Day watching the parade.

I hope the point is clearly made. Our goals are found outside of our comfort zone. Worthiness to receive is crucial. Knowing that giving and receiving are one in truth, we strengthen one by practicing the other. And the idea is strengthened in both ourselves and those with whom we exchange our gifts.

Know that you are deserving, worthy of receiving God's blessings, God's favor. We might think we deserve to stay at the Waldorf Astoria but feel absolutely uncomfortable there. This is where our stretching and growing will take place.

Check in with yourself to honestly appraise where you are on the continuum from fear to faith. And do not judge yourself harshly. It is a simple matter to gauge where we are and grow from there.

This Is Not the End

This finishes our twelve-weeks together, but this is not the end of your journey to greater and deeper prosperity and abundance. It is merely the start of a lifetime road leading up, out of the darkness and gloom, into the sunlight of the Spirit!

As you apply these lessons, practicing and believing with faith, something new and beautiful will emerge.

Looking back at something that might have terrified you, but that is now second nature, you will be amazed by your newfound comfort zone.

Recalling how you stretched, writing that first tithe check, you will come to see that tithing is something you cannot live without, not any more than you could live without food, air, or water.

You will meet and exceed your goals, while keeping your eye on the far horizon.

You will marvel at how far you have come.

You will wonder what greater good is in store for you in the days ahead.

More good is always in store for you, as long as you keep to the path and do things that work, following the laws of the Universe.

Ask what is yours to do. Claim your inheritance as a child of God! Work hand-in-hand with the Great Spirit of the Universe Who is your Partner, Friend, Parent, and Who loves you deeply and infinitely.

Trust God—I Am Prosperous!

Clean house—You Are Prosperous!

Help Others!—We Are Prosperous!

Thank You, God!

Use This New Tithing Affirmation

I have enough!
I have more than enough!
I have more than enough to share!
And, I am ready to receive more!

Tithe—*Divine Love, flowing through me, blesses and multiplies all that I have, all that I give and all that I receive. We are blessed to know that Spirit is our Source. God bless! Thank you, God!*

Sing

"I Am So Blessed"
by Karen Drucker

I Am so blessed
I Am so blessed
I Am so grateful, for all that I have
I Am so blessed, I Am so blessed
I Am so grateful, I Am so blessed

We are so blessed
We are so blessed
We are so grateful, for all that we have
We are so blessed, We are so blessed
We are so grateful, We are so blessed

God bless! Thank you, God!

Appendix

The Twelve Steps of Alcoholics Anonymous

1. We admitted we were powerless over alcohol—that our lives had become unmanageable.
2. Came to believe that a Power greater than ourselves could restore us to sanity.
3. Made a decision to turn our will and our lives over to the care of God as we understood Him.
4. Made a searching and fearless moral inventory of ourselves.
5. Admitted to God, to ourselves, and to another human being the exact nature of our wrongs.
6. Were entirely ready to have God remove all these defects of character.
7. Humbly asked Him to remove our shortcomings.
8. Made a list of all persons we had harmed, and became willing to make amends to them all.
9. Made direct amends to such people wherever possible, except when to do so would injure them or others.
10. Continued to take personal inventory and when we were wrong promptly admitted it.
11. Sought through prayer and meditation to improve our conscious contact with God, as we understood Him, praying only for knowledge of His will for us and the power to carry that out.
12. Having had a spiritual awakening as the result of these Steps, we tried to carry this message to alcoholics, and to practice these principles in all our affairs.

About the Author

John Frederick is—or has been—an author, poet, musician, photographer, travel guide, spiritual student, spiritual guide, father, grandfather, politician, chef, legislator, pool player, teacher, and pronoic dreamer.

His personal journey from addiction and homelessness to a life of prosperity and abundance, through the application of spiritual principles, has convinced him that it is never too late for anyone to wake up and live the life of their dreams.

He currently resides in Paris, France, with Manny and Erica, his two teacup Yorkies.

Book John to Speak at Your Next Event

John A. Frederick is an ordained Interfaith minister and spiritual tour guide available for individual sessions and group discussions, coaching, speaking engagements, seminars, weekly or weekend retreats, book clubs, media interviews, and other events.

Drawing on more than thirty years of personal experience in his own life-journey, through twelve-step recovery, studying metaphysics, pastoral counseling, dream-work, prosperity teaching, and walking spiritual paths to physical healing, John has a true "rags to-riches" story.

Starting in his teenage years, addictions slowly turned his life into one of desperation, loneliness, poverty, and hopelessness. Through the miracle of recovery and the discovery of metaphysical spiritual principles—spiritual laws that work in a practical way to heal past trauma, dissolve old ideas, and inspire new ideas and beliefs that are true and that work—John's life made a 180° turnaround.

A successful author, now healthy after several life-threatening illnesses, and living his dream in Paris, France, John can help you find your way to wholeness, prosperity, and success. Through the principles laid out in Prosperity Now! you can discover where your life has been, notice where it's headed, discern where your goals and dreams lie, and make a roadmap to find your way to a new, better, more abundant and prosperous life!

Helping you discover your passion and the joy of living is John's gift. In keeping with his motto, Vivez Joyeaux (Live Joyously) John's insights and techniques will enliven any event, inspire any audience, improve any circumstance, and give new direction to anyone who wants to live in Prosperity Now!

To discuss your individual or group's needs, contact him at:

prosperitynowlifeofdreams@yahoo.com

www.ingramcontent.com/pod-product-compliance
Lightning Source LLC
Chambersburg PA
CBHW071235070526
44583CB00017B/2194